BBC LEARN WELSH

GRAMMAR GUIDE

BBC
LEARN
WELSH

**The ideal aid to
speaking and writing**

**Up-to-date
and easy to use**

First impression: 2004

© BBC/ELWa and Y Lolfa Cyf., 2004

This publication and the BBC Learn Welsh website were produced in association with ELWa, the National Council for Education and Training for Wales

Published by Y Lolfa with the permission of the BBC

The BBC logo is a trade mark of the British Broadcasting Corporation and is used under licence. BBC logo © BBC 1996

Senior Development Manager ELWa: Einir Wyn Kirkwood
Content: Ann Jones, Meic Gilby
Editor: Geraint Hughes
Project Co-ordinator: Ian Grutchfield
Design Co-ordinator: Simon Rooney
Additional Material: Chris Reynolds

ISBN: 0 86243 730 x

Published and printed in Wales
by Y Lolfa Cyf., Talybont, Ceredigion SY24 5AP
e-mail ylolfa@ylolfa.com
website www.ylolfa.com
tel (01970) 832 304
fax 832 782

CONTENTS

Preface

BBC Wales has been broadcasting for over 80 years. An important part of the service is the production of television and radio programmes for learners of all levels and ages.

Learn Welsh is a new website for Welsh learners, capitalising on the success of the *Catchphrase* radio series. One of the most popular features of *Learn Welsh* is the *Language Tools* facility, which includes an online grammar guide. In response to numerous requests for this resource to be available in printed form, I am pleased to present a pocket-sized grammar guide.

I am grateful for the ongoing assistance of ELWa, the National Council for Education and Learning for Wales, who have supported this publication.

I hope you will find the guide useful as you become proficient in the language.

For details of other resources available please visit our website: www.bbc.co.uk/learnwelsh

Eleri Wyn Lewis
Head of Education and Learning
BBC Wales

1

THE ALPHABET

1 The Alphabet

1.1 The Alphabet

a b c ch d dd e f ff g ng h i j l ll m n o p ph r rh s t th u w y

- The traditional Welsh alphabet consists of twenty eight letters, based on the Roman alphabet. In addition, the letter **j** has been borrowed in words such as **jam**, **jôc** and **garej**, though not all Welsh alphabets you see may recognize this.

- Welsh is a phonetic language, which means that every letter is always pronounced. There are no silent letters (for example, the English knight, psychology, fore) or alternative pronunciations (cough, Slough, ghoul).

- When you become proficient enough in the language to attempt crosswords, remember that the digraphs **ch**, **dd**, **ff**, **ng**, **ll**, **ph**, **rh** and **th** are single letters in Welsh as they are representing a single sound. Thus **chwech** (six) only has 4 letters in Welsh! This also has implications when using a dictionary: **angel** (angel) comes before **anabl** (disabled) in Welsh because the letter **ng** comes before **n** in the alphabet.

- The stress in Welsh words falls regularly on the last but one syllable (for example, **Llanélli**, **Abertáwe**), but there are a few exceptions, most notably the word for Welsh, **Cymraeg**, which is accented on the last syllable.

1.2 Pronunciation

Letter	Pronunciation	Example
a	hard, ham, but never as in same	**afal** (apple)
b	boy	**bachgen** (boy)
c	cow, but never as in circumstance	**coch** (red)
ch	loch, Bach, but never as in poach	**chwech** (six)
d	down	**dau** (two)
dd	them, but never as in udder	**deuddeg** (twelve)
e	sane, self	**eliffant** (elephant)
f	very, but never as in fairly	**fi** (me)
ff	fairy	**ffa** (beans)
g	garden, but never as in gorge	**gwyn** (white)
ng	king, never as in angel somtimes as in anger	**angor** (anchor) **Bangor**
h	head	**hedfan** (fly)
i	tea, but never as in time	**trin** (treat)
j	jam	**jam** (jam)
l	low	**lawnt** (lawn)
ll	**Ll, ll** – as in **Ll**ane**ll**i This sound does not occur in English, and is the one sound which gives problems to newcomers to the Welsh language. Place the tongue on the roof of the mouth behind the teeth as if to pronounce l, then blow voicelessly	**llaw** (hand)
m	mine	**mam** (mother)
n	nanny	**naw** (nine)
o	ore, pond, but never as in moan, only	**coch** (red)
p	pine	**pump** (five)
ph	photography	**ei pherlau** (her pearls)
r	more rolled in Welsh – as in **rh**apsody, **rh**ombus	**roced** (rocket)
rh	aspirated r, as in per**h**aps	**rhaw** (spade)
s	sort, but never as in as	**saith** (seven)
t	tree	**tri** (three)
th	theory, but never as in them	**saith** (seven)
u	green in South Wales, but in north Wales is more akin to the French **u**	**un** (one)
w	do, look	**cwm** (valley)
y	her, flea, fin, fun	**ynys** (island)

1.3 Consonants

● The consonants **dd**, **ng**, **ph**, **th** do not occur at the beginning of Welsh words unless they are being mutated. There is an explanation of this phenomenon in Section 3.

● The letters **i** and **w** sometimes perform the functions of consonants in Welsh, with **i** resembling the **y** in youth and **w** the clipped **w** in water.

● The combination **gwl-** as in **gwlyb** (wet) is pronounced as a cluster of consonants: sound the **g**, form the **w** but sound the **l**. The combined actions of lips, tongue and voice will give you the correct sound. Because of the consonantal nature of the **w**, the word **gwlyb** has only one syllable.

● There is no **k**, **q**, **v**, **x** or **z** in Welsh and these sounds are represented by other letters or a combination of letters (**c**, **cw**, **f**, **cs**).

● **Z** does not occur as a sound in Welsh.

● There's no letter to represent the English **ch** sound in Welsh, initially as in **ch**ocolate and **Ch**ina, or finally as in wat**ch**: the sound does exist in borrowed words, but it is represented by combinations of letters which approximate the original sound. For example:

English	Welsh
chocolate	siocled
China	Tseina
watch	wats
chips	tships

1.4 Vowels

● The vowels in Welsh are **a**, **e**, **i**, **o**, **u**, **w** and **y**, and they can be short or long:

Short		Long	
a	as in pat	â, a	as in father
e	as in red	ê, e	as in shale
i	as in hit	î, i	as in heat
o	as in hot	ô, o	as in oar
u	as in hint	û, u	as in steed
w	as in book	ŵ, w	as in move
y	as in sit	ŷ, y	as in seat

The length of a vowel is determined by the consonant or cluster of syllables which follow.

● Open-ended vowels in words of one syllable are long:

da	good	du	black
de	south	nhw	they, them
ti	you (familiar)	fy	my
do	yes (past tense)	tŷ	house

● Words consisting only of one vowel are short:

a	and	**o**	from
e	he, him	**y**	the
i	to		

● **a, e, i, o, w** are short before **c, ng, p, t,** and before clusters of consonants:

llong	ship
twt	tidy, small
het	hat

● **a, e, i, o, u, w** are long before **b, ch, d, dd, f, ff, s, th**:

coch	red
haf `	summer
llid	inflammation

● **a, e, i, o, u, w** can be short or long before **l, n, r**:

lol	nonsense (pronounced as in lolly)	gôl	goal
her	challenge	mêr	marrow
llan	church	cân	song
prin	scarce	gwin	wine

● **u** is short before clusters of consonants:

punt	pound
pump	five

- **u** is long before **b, ch, d, dd, f, ff, l, ll, n, r, s, th**:

mud	dumb
sudd	juice
cul	narrow
llun	picture

- **y** is short before clusters:

gwynt	wind
tyst	witness

- **y** is long before **b, ch, d, dd, g, s, th**:

tyb	opinion
sych	dry

- long or short before **l, n, r**:

llyn	lake
cŷn	chisel

1.5 Vowel combinations (diphthongs)

- There are no diphthongs as in English; that is, two vowels used to produce one sound (as in friend, cheat, pour, coot).

- All vowels are pronounced separately, in rapid succession.

- The phonetic nature of the language means that you will come across three vowels together (**caead** – lid, **tawel** – silent), four vowels together (**neiaint** – nephews, **gwaywffon** – spear) or even five vowels together (**gloywais** – I shone, **gweuais** – I knitted).

1.6 Differences between English and Welsh

Grammatically, there are some basic differences between Welsh and English. It would be well to note those differences at the outset.

● There is no indefinite article in Welsh.

bachgen	a boy, boy
merch	a girl, girl

● All nouns are either masculine or feminine and must be translated **e/fe** or **hi** according to gender.

● The gender of a noun often determines the form of many dependent words: it may cause a mutation, take a mutation, require a feminine/masculine adjective, need a gender specific pronoun.

● The adjective usually follows the noun.

bachgen bach	small boy

● Adjectival numbers are followed by a singular noun

tri bachgen	three boys

● Normally, the verb stands at the beginning of the clause/sentence.

Mae'r dynion yn y capel	The men are in the chapel

2

GRAMMATICAL TERMS EXPLAINED

2 Grammatical terms explained

Some of the terms used in this book may not be familiar to you. This section explains these terms in alphabetical order:

Adjective   Ansoddair
A word that modifies a noun or pronoun by describing a particular characteristic of it. In Welsh, they usually come after the noun/pronoun. In this example **da** is the adjective:

Bachgen da ydy John	John is a good boy

Adverb   Adferf
A word that modifies a verb, an adjective, another adverb, a preposition, a phrase, a clause or a sentence, and that answers such questions as how/why/with whom/when/where. A clause which does this is called an adverbial clause. In this example **tawel** is the adverb:

Mae hi'n siarad yn dawel	She's talking quietly

Article   Y Fannod
In the case of English, this is a word which gives a noun definiteness or indefiniteness. In Welsh, there is only a definite article, which takes the form **y** (between consonants), **yr** (before vowel) and **'r** (after vowel). In this example **'r** is the definite article:

Mae'r bachgen yn dda	The boy is good

Clause   Cymal
Third largest unit of grammatical organisation which can be part of, or a whole, sentence. There are four types in Welsh:

Dyna'r dyn a welais i ddoe	There's the man whom I saw yesterday (Adjectival)
Dyna'r ferch a ganodd ddoe	There's the girl who sang yesterday (Relative)
Clywais i fod y ferch yn canu	I heard that the girl is singing (Noun)
Dewch yn ôl pan glywch chi'r gloch yn canu	Come back when you hear the bell ringing (Adverbial)

Conjugation   Rhediad

A system of verbal inflections which, in Welsh, give the person, tense and mood of the verb. The conjugation of the Perfect Tense, Indicative Mood of the verb 'to watch' is:

Gwyliais i	Gwylion ni
Gwyliaist ti	Gwylioch chi
Gwyliodd e/hi	Gwylion nhw

Emphasis   Pwyslais

Stress laid on a word or phrase to give it special or prominent meaning. In Welsh this can be done a number of ways, for example, changing word order, using modifiers or using special forms of the verb. In the example:

Bachgen mawr ydy e	He's a big boy

bachgen mawr is being emphasised

Genitive   Genidol

Denotes a relationship and sometimes ownership, for example:

cadair y bardd	the poet's chair
gwallt merch	a girl's hair, girl's hair
fy nghar	my car
diwedd y ffilm	the end of the film

Idiom   Priod-ddull, Idiom

An expression unique to a language, which can lose its true meaning or simply doesn't make sense in translation, for example:

Mae'n bwrw hen wragedd a ffyn

Literally translated:	It's raining old women and sticks
Means:	It's raining very heavily

Rydw i wrth fy modd yn gwrando ar Gôr Meibion Dyfnant

Literally translated:	I am in my element listening to Dunvant Male Choir
Means:	I really enjoy listening to the Dunvant Male Choir

Impersonal   Amhersonol

A verb ending which denotes action and time but which does not give information about person(s) carrying out the action. Orally, the idea is conveyed by **cael** (have), for example:

| Mae'r tŷ wedi cael ei werthu | The house has been sold |

In more formal Welsh the endings are:

-id (imperfect)	Gwerthid llyfrau yma	Books were sold here (over a long period)
-wyd (past perfect)	Gwerthwyd llyfrau yma	Books were sold here
-ir (present/future)	Gwerthir llyfrau yma	Books are sold here

Long forms/Periphrastic forms   Ffurfiau Hir

Sentences which use a form of the verb-noun 'to be' to create the verb, usually following the pattern:

| to be **Mae** | + | person **John** | + | **yn** **yn** | + | predicate **mynd** |

Modify   Goleddfu

To qualify or expand the meaning of a word by using other words. In the example:

| Mae'n dwym iawn heddiw | It's very warm today |

iawn is modifying **twym**

Mood   Modd

Forms of the verb which indicate whether a statement, command or wish is being expressed. The three moods in Welsh are:

INDICATIVE	expresses a fact or a statement	Mae John yn eistedd John is sitting
SUBJUNCTIVE	expresses a wish or something conditional	Buasai John yn eistedd John would sit
IMPERATIVE	expresses a command or strong desire or invitation	Eisteddwch, John! Sit down, John!

Mutation **Treiglad**

A consonant change usually at the beginning of a word which occurs because of a word or phrase preceding it.

Noun **Enw**

A word used to represent someone or something about which you are talking. In Welsh, all nouns are either feminine, masculine or plural. In this example **merch** is the noun:

Merch ydy hi	She's a girl

Object **Gwrthrych**

The focus of the action being carried out in a sentence. The object can be a noun, pronoun or noun phrase. In this example **llyfr** is the object:

Prynais i lyfr	I bought a book

Parenthesis **Sangiad**

A break in the normal run of a phrase or clause by something connected but non-essential. In this example **fel oedd ei arfer** is the parenthesis:

Edrychai, fel oedd ei arfer, yn ŵr bonheddig	He looked, as he usually did, a gentleman

Particle **Geiryn**

A figure of speech which is not mutated and which cannot be used by itself, for example: **y, yr, na, nad, nid, ai, oni**.

Person **Person**

The grammatical term referring to one of three classes, in either the singular or the plural, usually with particular reference to who is carrying out an action. When the conjugations of a verb are given, they are always in the same order:

1st person singular	me	1st person plural	us
2nd person singular	you	2nd person plural	you
3rd person singular	him/her/noun	3rd person plural	them

Predicate   **Traethiad**

The thing which is being said about the subject of the sentence. In this example the verb-noun **mynd** is the predicate:

Mae John yn mynd	John is going

In this example the adjective **twp** is the predicate:

Mae John yn dwp	John is stupid

Preposition   **Arddodiad**

Words which express a relationship to another word or element, for example:

> **am** (of), **ar** (on), **at** (to), **gan** (by), **heb** (without), **hyd** (until), **i** (to), **o dan** (under), **tan** (until), **dros** (over), **drwy** (through), **wrth** (by)

Pronoun   **Rhagenw**

Words which represent a noun. There are three types in Welsh:

Independent	(mi, ti, ef)
Dependent	(fy, dy, 'w, 'th)
Relative	(a, y/yr)

Question words   **Geirynnau holi**

Words used at the beginning of a sentence to form a question. Most can be used by themselves to gain further information. Examples of question words are: **beth** (what), **pwy** (who), **ble** (where), **pam** (why), **faint/sawl** (how many), **pa** (which), **pryd** (when).

Short forms/concise forms   **Ffurfiau byr/cryno**

Endings can be added to the stems of verb-nouns to show person and tense. Both of the following examples can be translated as 'I'm going to the cinema':

Rydw i'n mynd i'r sinema	(Long Form)
Af i'r sinema	(Short Form)

Subject   **Goddrych**

The subject is the person or noun completing the action expressed by the verb in a sentence. In this example **y bachgen** is the subject:

Rhedodd y bachgen dros y sir	The boy ran for the county

In Welsh, the personal endings can denote the subject without any need for a noun or pronoun:

Rhed_odd_ dros y sir	**He/she** ran for the county

Tense   **Amser**

This is the form taken by the verb to indicate when the action took place. The tenses are:

PRESENT	actions occurring now	I am
PRESENT HABITUAL	actions which usually occur	I usually do
PRESENT PERFECT	actions which have occurred	I have
PRESENT PERFECT CONTINUOUS	actions which have been occurring	I have been
IMPERFECT	actions which were occurring	I was
IMPERFECT CONTINUOUS	actions which used to occur	I used to
PLUPERFECT TENSE	actions which had occurred	I had
PLUPERFECT CONTINUOUS TENSE	actions which had been occurring	I had been
PAST TENSE	actions which occurred	I did
FUTURE TENSE	actions which will occur	I will
FUTURE PERFECT	actions which will have occurred	I will have
FUTURE PERFECT CONTINUOUS	actions which will have been occurring	I will have been

2 Grammatical terms explained

Verb   **Berf**

A word used to indicate an action, state or occurrence. In this example
siaradodd is the verb:

Siaradodd hi'n dawel	She spoke quietly

Verb-noun   **Berfenw**

A combination of a verb and a noun which gives an action its name, not unlike
the infinitive in English. In Welsh, every action is a verb-noun until it is either
placed with a verb formed from 'to be' or an ending is added to it. **Cael** (have),
rhedeg (run), **gwisgo** (wear) are examples of verb-nouns.

3

BEGINNERS

3.1 The Article

● There is no indefinite article (a/an) in Welsh, for example:

cath	a cat	afal	an apple
merch	a girl	ysgol	a school

● There are three forms of the definite article (the) in Welsh:

(1) **y** is used in front of a consonant. Singular, feminine nouns will undergo a Soft Mutation after **y** (except those beginning with **ll** and **rh**):

ci	y ci	the dog
cath	y gath	the cat
bachgen	y bachgen	the boy
merch	y ferch	the girl

(2) **yr** is used in front of a vowel and in front of h. Remember that **w** and **y** are vowels in Welsh:

ysgol	yr ysgol	the school
enw	yr enw	the name
afal	yr afal	the apple
het	yr het	the hat

(3) **'r** is used after a word ending in a vowel no matter whether the word which follows begins with a vowel or with a consonant:

Mae'r plant	The children are
Mae'r ysgol	The school is
Dyma'r llyfr	Here's the book
Dacw'r afon	There's the river

3.2 Nouns

All nouns in Welsh are either masculine or feminine. Unfortunately there is no way of telling which nouns are feminine and which are masculine, so it is important to learn the gender at the same time as the meaning. In a dictionary **b** (**benywaidd**) or **f** (**feminine**) will denote feminine nouns and **g** (**gwrywaidd**) or **m** (**masculine**) will denote masculine nouns.

● Singular, feminine nouns undergo a Soft Mutation after the definite article **y** (the) (except those words which begin with **ll** and **rh**):

tref	y dref	the town
cadair	y gadair	the chair
merch	y ferch	the girl
llaw	y llaw	the hand
rhaw	y rhaw	the spade

● We always use singular nouns after numbers in Welsh. Although the plural of **car** is **ceir**, note the use of the singular form after numbers:

one car	un car	ten cars	deg car
eight cars	wyth car	two cars	dau gar

● Feminine nouns undergo a Soft Mutation after the numbers **un** (one) (except those words which begin with **ll** and **rh**) and **dwy** (two). Notice that the form **dwy** is used with feminine nouns only:

un ferch	one girl	dwy ferch	two girls
un llaw	one hand	dwy law	two hands
un bont	one bridge	dwy bont	two bridges

● Masculine nouns undergo a Soft Mutation after the number **dau** (two). Notice that the form **dau** is used with masculine nouns only:

dau fachgen	two boys	dau gi	two dogs
dau ddyn	two men	dau gar	two cars

● Masculine nouns after **tri** (three) and all singular nouns after **chwe** (six) undergo an Aspirate Mutation. The form **tri** is used with masculine nouns only:

tri cheffyl	three horses
tri phlentyn	three children
tri thractor	three tractors
chwe cheiniog	six pennies (pence)
chwe phunt	six pounds
chwe thegan	six toys

● Nouns will undergo a Soft Mutation after the linking **yn**:

Roedd Mair yn ddoctor	Mair was a doctor
Mae e'n filiwnydd (S.W.)*	He's a millionaire
Dydy o ddim yn brifathro (N.W.)*	He isn't a headmaster

(S.W.)* - South Wales, (N.W.)* - North Wales

3.3 Adjectives

● Nearly all adjectives follow the noun in Welsh:

bachgen bach	a small/little boy
car mawr	a big/large car
mynydd uchel	a high mountain
ffilm hir	a long film

● There are a few exceptions to this rule – **hen** (old), **hoff** (favourite) and **prif** (main/chief) are three of them:

hen ddyn	an old man
hoff fwyd	favourite food
prif gymeriad	main character

You will notice that placed before in front of the noun they cause the noun to undergo a Soft Mutation.

● When an adjective follows a singular, feminine noun it undergoes a Soft Mutation:

merch fach	a little girl
cadair fawr	a large chair
siop ddiddorol	an interesting shop
ysgol dda	a good school

● Sometimes another noun can be used as an adjective or a descriptive word:

siop fara	bread shop (bakers)
siop gig	meat shop (butchers)

● When an adjective stands alone in a sentence (i.e. it doesn't stand next to the noun it describes) the linking word **yn** is used in front of it:

Mae'r bws yn gynnar	The bus is early
Dydy'r car ddim yn hen	The car isn't old
Roedd y plant yn oer	The children were cold

● This word **yn** causes the adjective to undergo a Soft Mutation:

Mae'r castell yn fawr	The castle is big
Mae'r ffilm yn ddiddorol	The film is interesting
Roedden ni'n boeth	We were hot

● We can qualify our adjectives by placing **rhy** (too), **gweddol** (quite/fairly), **eitha** (quite/fairly) or **lled** (quite/fairly) between **yn** and the adjective. **Gweddol** will undergo a Soft Mutation after **yn** but **rhy** and **lled** will not (as **rh** and **ll** are exceptions to the rule). The full form of **eitha** is **eithaf** but the final **f** is normally dropped in the spoken language. This happens in most words which end in **f**. All except **eitha** cause the adjective which follows to undertake a Soft Mutation:

yn weddol ddiddorol	fairly interesting
yn rhy boeth	too hot
yn lled dal	quite tall
yn eitha tew	quite fat

3.3.1 Comparison of adjectives

As in English there are three methods of comparing adjectives in Welsh.

● The largest group is that to which appropriate endings are added, as in these examples using **tal** (tall), and **coch** (red):

tall	as tall as	taller than	the tallest
tal	mor dal â	yn dalach na	y tala (m + pl)/ y dala (f)
red	as red as	redder than	the reddest
coch	mor goch â	yn gochach na	y cocha (m + pl)/ y gocha (f)

● The equative degree (as … as) can also be formed by adding the ending **ed** to these short adjectives and by placing the word **cyn** in front:

mor dal â   cyn daled â
mor goch â   cyn goched â

● Notice the Soft Mutation after **mor** and **cyn**. Note also that we do not place **yn** in front of either **mor** or **cyn**:

Mae hi mor dal â fi
Mae hi cyn daled â fi

● Notice the Soft Mutation after **yn/'n**:

Mae hi'n dalach na fi
Mae fodca yn gryfach na gwin

● Notice the Soft Mutation after **y** in the superlative degree when it refers to a feminine noun.

John oedd y tala
Ann oedd y dala

● Notice the Aspirate Mutation after both **â** and **na**:

mor dal â choeden/   as tall as a tree
cyn daled â choeden
yn gochach na thân   redder than fire

● You will notice a change of spelling in some adjectives when endings are added to them:

w > y	trwm (heavy)	cyn drymed â	yn drymach na	y tryma
d > t	drud (expensive)	cyn ddruted â	yn ddrutach na	y druta
g > c	pwysig (important)	cyn bwysiced â	yn bwysicach na	y pwysica
b > p	gwlyb (wet)	cyn wlyped a	yn wlypach na	y gwlypa

● Some adjectives are too long to accommodate endings. Most of them end in -**ol**, -**og**, -**us** or -**gar**, but not all.

interesting	as interesting as	more interesting than '	the most interesting
diddorol	mor ddiddorol â	yn fwy diddorol na (m + pl)	y mwya diddorol diddorol (m + pl) y fwyaf diddorol (f)
tasty	as tasty as	tastier than	the tastiest
blasus	mor flasus â	yn fwy blasus na	y mwya blasus (m + pl); y fwya blasus (f)

You will notice long Welsh adjectives are not necessarily long in English and vice versa.

● One or two adjectives will follow this pattern although they are short:

swil (shy)	mor swil â	yn fwy swil na	mwya swil (m + pl) y fwya swil (f)

Also: **gwyllt** (wild), **diflas** (miserable, boring), **gwyntog** (windy)

3.3.2 Irregular adjectives

The following are the main irregular adjectives:

big great much	as big as as great as as much as	bigger than greater than more than	the biggest the greatest the most
mawr	cymaint â	yn fwy na	y mwya (m + pl)/ y fwya (f)
small little	as small as as little as	smaller than less than	the smallest the least
bach	cyn lleied â	yn llai na	y lleia (m + f + pl)
good	as good as	better than	the best
da	cystal â	yn well na	y gorau (m + pl)/ yr orau (f)
bad	as bad as	worse than	the worst
drwg	cynddrwg â	yn waeth na	y gwaetha (m + pl)/ y waetha (f)
high	as high as	higher than	the highest
uchel	cyfuwch â	yn uwch na	yr ucha (m + f +pl)
low	as low as	lower than	the lowest
isel	cyn ised â	yn is na	yr isa (m + f + pl)
near	as near as	nearer than	the nearest
agos	cyn agosed â	yn nes na	yr agosa (m + f + pl)

● In the equative degree the following forms are also acceptable:

cymaint â	mor fawr â
cyn lleied â	mor fach â
cynddrwg â	mor ddrwg â
cyfuwch â	mor uchel â
cyn ised â	mor isel â
cyn agosed â	mor agos â

● In the comparative degree the following form is also acceptable:

yn nes na	yn agosach na

● Notice that we use **â** and **na** in front of words which begin with a consonant and **ag** and **nag** in front of words which begin with a vowel:

cyn dewed ag eliffant	as fat as an elephant
yn fwy cymylog na ddoe	cloudier than yesterday
yn fwy cymylog nag echdoe	cloudier than the day before yesterday

● There is an Aspirate Mutation after both **â** and **na**:

mor fynyddig â Chymru	as mountainous as Wales
yn dalach na choeden	taller than a tree

● Sentences containing either the comparative and equative degree follow the normal sentence pattern, with the verb at the beginning of the sentence:

Mae'r llyfrgell mor bell (cyn belled) â'r orsaf	The library is as far as the station
Ydy tŷ Tom cymaint â thŷ Bill?	Is Tom's house as big as Bill's house?
Roedd Tom yn dalach na Bill	Tom was taller than Bill
Mae'r ferch yn dewach na'r bachgen	The girl is fatter than the boy

● But when we use the superlative degree of the adjective we must use the emphatic pattern, i.e. the verb doesn't come at the beginning of the sentence:

Efrog Newydd ydy'r pella	New York is the farthest
Castell Harlech ydy'r mwya ym Mhrydain?	Harlech Castle is the largest in Britain?
Muhammad Ali oedd y gorau	Muhammad Ali was the best

● Note that the verb will always be in the third person singular:

Fi ydy'r gorau	I am the best
Chi ydy'r tala	You are the tallest
Nhw ydy'r gwaetha	They are the worst
Nhw oedd y gwaetha	They were the worst

● In English we cannot use the superlative degree when comparing only two things. We must use the comparative degree:

Tom and Paul. Tom is the taller. (not 'tallest')

This rule doesn't apply in Welsh:

Tom a Paul. Tom ydy'r tala

3.4 Prepositions

● **ar** (on) is followed by a Soft Mutation:

bwrdd y gegin	ar fwrdd y gegin	on the kitchen table
llong	ar long	on a ship

● **ar** has personal forms:

arna i	arnon ni
arnat ti	arnoch chi
arno fe (S.W.)	arnyn nhw
arno fo (N.W.)	
arni hi	

● **i** (to) and **o** (from/of) are followed by a Soft Mutation.

O Gaergybi i Gaerdydd	From Holyhead to Cardiff
O Ddolgellau i Bontypridd	From Dolgellau to Pontypridd
Llun o Gastell Harlech	A picture of Harlech Castle

- **i** has personal forms:

i mi/fi	i ni
i ti	i chi
iddo fe (S.W.)	iddyn nhw
iddo fo (N.W.)	
iddi hi	

- **i** is used in the **rhaid** (must) pattern:

Mae rhaid iddyn nhw golli pwysau	They must lose weight
Oes rhaid iddo fo (N.W.) fynd	Does he have to go to the dentist?
at y deintydd?	

- **o** has personal forms:

ohono i	ohonon ni
ohonot ti	ohonoch chi
ohono fe (S.W.)	ohonyn nhw
ohono fo (N.W.)	
ohoni hi	
Dyma rai ohonyn nhw	Here are some of them
Wyt ti wedi gweld llun ohoni hi?	Have you seen a photograph of her?

- **am** (about/for) is followed by a Soft Mutation:

am ddau fis	for two months
	(**dau** is used with a masculine noun)
am bedair blynedd	for four years
	(**pedair** is used with a feminine noun)

- **am** has personal forms:

amdana i	amdanon ni
amdanat ti	amdanoch chi
amdano fe (S.W.)	amdanyn nhw
amdano fo (N.W.)	
amdani hi	

- **am** is used after certain verbs. Here are five:

aros am	to wait for
chwilio am	to search for
edrych am	to look for/to visit
siarad am	to talk about
poeni am	to worry about

For example,

Maen nhw'n siarad amdanoch chi	They're talking about you
Wyt ti'n poeni amdani hi?	Are you worrying about her?

- **at** (to/towards) is followed by a Soft Mutation:

at ddrws yr ystafell	to the door of the room
at reolwr y siop	to the manager of the shop

- **at** has personal forms:

ata i	aton ni
atat ti	atoch chi
ato fe (S.W.)	atyn nhw
ato fo (N.W.)	
ati hi	

- **at** is used after certain verbs. Here are three:

ysgrifennu at	to write to
anfon at	to send to
cofio at	to remember to

For example:

Wyt ti'n mynd i ysgrifennu ati hi?	Are you going to write to her?
Dw i wedi anfon llythyr atyn nhw	I have sent them a letter

● **gan** (with) also has personal forms in different dialects, and the various forms can sound slightly different in pronunciation:

gen i	gynnon ni
gen ti	gynnoch chi
gan Siân/gynni hi	gynnyn nhw
gan y plant/gan Siôn/	
gynno fo	

In North Wales these forms are used in the possession pattern. Notice that the verb at the beginning is always in the 3rd person singular (**mae/roedd**) and that noun which follows the pattern undergoes a Soft Mutation:

Mae gen i gath	I've got a cat
Roedd gen i ddau gi	I had two dogs

Notice the spoken forms of the negative pattern in North Wales:

Does gen i ddim	Sgen i ddim
Does gen ti ddim	Sgen ti ddim
Does gan Tom ddim	Sgan Tom ddim
Does gynno fo ddim	Sgynno fo ddim
Does gynni hi ddim	Sgynni hi ddim
Does gynnon ni ddim	Sgynnon ni ddim
Does gynnoch chi ddim	Sgynnoch chi ddim
Does gynnon nhw ddim	Sgynnyn nhw ddim

Notice the spoken forms of the question pattern in North Wales:

Oes gen i?	Sgen i?
Oes gen ti?	Sgen ti?
Oes gan Tom?	Sgan Tom?
Oes gynno fo?	Sgynno fo?
Oes gynni hi?	Sgynni hi?
Oes gynnon ni?	Sgynnon ni?
Oes gynnoch chi?	Sgynnoch chi?
Oes gynnon nhw?	Sgynnyn nhw?

● In South Wales the following pattern is normally used:

Mae car gyda fi	I have a car
Does dim ci gyda Tom	Tom doesn't have a dog

● **gyda** is often abbreviated to **'da**, especially in speech:

Mae car 'da fi	I have a car
Does dim ci 'da Tom	Tom doesn't have a dog

● **yn** (in) causes a Nasal Mutation:

Dolgellau	yn Nolgellau
tŷ Bob	yn nhŷ Bob

● **yn** changes to **ym** if the word which follows it begins with an **m**:

Bangor	ym Mangor
parc y dref	ym mharc y dref

● **yn** changes to **yng** if the word which follows it begins with **ng**:

Gardd Eden	yng Ngardd Eden
Cymru	yng Nghymru

● Don't confuse **mewn** (in a) with **yn** (in) or **yn y** (in the):

mewn tŷ	in a house	yn y tŷ	in the house
mewn car	in a car	yn y car	in the car

● We all know that it is considered grammatically incorrect to end a sentence with a preposition in English (but we often hear such sentences in the spoken language), for example:

This is the house I live in	(...in which I live)
Who are you talking about?	(About whom are you talking?)

This rule does not apply in Welsh so long as the personal form of the preposition is used:

Dyma'r tŷ dw i'n byw ynddo	This is the house I live in
Pwy ydy'r plant rydyn ni'n gwrando arnyn nhw?	Who are the children we are listening to?
Pwy oedd y ferch roedden nhw'n edrych amdani?	Who was the girl they were looking for?

3.5 Verbs (long forms)

3.5.1 Present Tense

● All verb-nouns are added to various persons of the verb to be linked by **yn**. There is no mutation after this linking **yn**.

● **Affirmative forms**

Standard forms	Spoken forms	English
Rydw i	Dw i	I am/do
Rwyt ti		You are/do
Mae e (S.W.) Mae o (N.W.)		He is/does
Mae hi		She is/does
Mae Tom		Tom is/does
Rydyn ni	'Dyn ni (S.W.)/ 'Dan ni (N.W.)	We are/do
Rydych chi	'Dych chi (S.W.)/ 'Dach chi (N.W.)	You are/do
Maen nhw		They are/do

For example:

Dw i'n byw yn Llandudno	I am living in Llandudno

● This is the literal translation of the Welsh sentence. It can also convey

I live in Llandudno
I do live in Llandudno

Common sense will tell you which version to use in a particular context.

- The singular form of the verb is used with all nouns, even with plural nouns:

Mae'r plant yn mynd i'r ysgol ar y bws	The children are going to school on the bus/The children go to school on the bus
Mae'r staff yn gweithio'n hwyr	The staff are working late

● Negative forms

Standard forms	Spoken forms	English
Dydw i ddim	Dw i ddim	I am not/do not
Dwyt ti ddim		You aren't/don't
Dydy e ddim (S.W.)/ Dydy o ddim (N.W.)	'Dyw e ddim (S.W.)/ 'Dy o ddim (N.W.)	He isn't/doesn't
Dydy hi ddim	'Dyw hi ddim (S.W.)/ 'Dy hi ddim (N.W.)	She isn't/doesn't
Dydy Tom ddim	'Dyw Tom ddim (S.W.)/ 'Dy Tom ddim (N.W.)	Tom isn't/doesn't
Dydyn ni ddim	'Dyn ni ddim (S.W.)/ 'Dan ni ddim (N.W.)	We aren't/don't
Dydych chi ddim	'Dych chi ddim(S.W.)/ 'Dach chi ddim (N.W.)	You aren't/don't
Dydyn nhw ddim	'Dyn nhw ddim (S.W.)/ 'Dan nhw ddim (N.W.)	They aren't/don't

For example:

Dydy hi ddim yn siopa yn Llundain	She isn't shopping in London She doesn't shop in London
'Dych/'Dach chi ddim yn gweithio'n galed	You aren't working hard You don't work hard
Dw i ddim yn byw yn Llandudno	I am not living in Llandudno I don't live in Llandudno
Dydy'r plant ddim yn chwarae pêl-droed yn y parc	The children are not playing football in the park The children don't play football in the park

- Notice that the linking word **yn** follows **ddim** in the negative.

● **Question and Answer forms**

Standard forms	Spoken forms	English	Answer
Ydw i?	Dw i?	Am/Do I?	(Nac) Wyt (familiar) /Ydych (polite)
Wyt ti?		Are/Do you? (familiar)	(Nac) Ydw
Ydy e (S.W.)/ Ydy o (N.W.)?		Is/Does he?	(Nac) Ydy
Ydy hi?		Is/Does she?	(Nac) Ydy
Ydy Tom?		Is/Does Tom?	(Nac) Ydy
Ydyn ni?	'Dyn ni? (S.W.)/ 'Dan ni? (N.W.)	Are/Do we?	(Nac) Ydyn
Ydych chi?	'Dych chi? (S.W.)/ 'Dach chi? (N.W.)	Are/Do you?	(Nac) Ydych
Ydyn nhw?	'Dyn nhw? (S.W.)/ 'Dan nhw? (N.W.)	Are/Do they?	(Nac) Ydyn

For example:

Ydy hi'n siopa yn Llundain? Ydy	Is she shopping in London? Yes (she is) Does she shop in London? Yes (she does)
'Dych chi'n gweithio'n galed? Nac ydw	Are you working hard? No (I'm not) Do you work hard? No (I don't)
Dw i'n byw yn Llandudno? Wyt/Ydych	Am I living in Llandudno? Yes (you are) Do I live in Llandudno? – Yes (you do)
Ydy'r plant yn cerdded i'r ysgol? Ydyn	Are the children walking to school? Yes (they are) Do the children walk to school? Yes (they do)

● **Indefinite forms**

Mae	There is/are
Does dim	There isn't/aren't
Oes? (answer Nac oes – No/	Is there/Are there?
Oes – Yes)	

For example:

Mae ci yn eistedd wrth y drws	There is a dog sitting by the door
Mae plant yn chwarae yn y parc	There are children playing in the park
Does dim ci yn eistedd wrth y drws	There isn't a dog sitting by the door
Does dim plant yn chwarae yn y parc	There aren't children playing in the park
Oes ci yn eistedd wrth y drws? Oes	Is there a dog sitting by the door? Yes
Oes plant yn chwarae yn y parc? Nac oes	Are there children playing in the park? No

● In North Wales the word **'na** is placed after **Mae/Oes?** and **Does**. As you can see in the following examples it causes a Soft Mutation.

Mae 'na gi yn eistedd wrth y drws	There is a dog sitting by the door
Oes 'na gi yn eistedd wrth y drws? Oes	Is there a dog sitting by the door? Yes
Does 'na ddim ci yn eistedd wrth y drws	There isn't a dog sitting by the door

3.5.2 Imperfect Tense

As in the Present Tense, all verb-nouns are added to various persons of the Imperfect Tense of the verb to be linked again by **yn**. There is no mutation after this linking **yn**.

● **Affirmative forms**

Standard forms	Spoken forms	English
Roeddwn i	Ron i	I was
Roeddet ti	Rot ti	You were
Roedd e (S.W.) Roedd o (N.W.)		He was
Roedd hi		She was
Roedd Tom		Tom was
Roedden ni	Ron ni	We were
Roeddech chi	Roch chi	You were
Roedden nhw	Ron nhw	They were

For example:

Roeddwn i'n byw yn Llandudno	I was living in Llandudno
Roeddech chi'n gweithio'n galed	You were working hard
Roedd hi'n siopa yn Llundain	She was shopping in London

● Notice that the singular form of the verb is used with all nouns, even with plural nouns:

Roedd y llyfrau ar y bwrdd	The books were on the table

● **Negative forms**

Standard forms	Spoken forms	English
Doeddwn i ddim	Don i ddim	I wasn't
Doeddet ti ddim	Dot ti ddim	You weren't
Doedd e ddim (S.W.)/ Doedd o ddim (N.W.)		He wasn't
Doedd hi ddim		She wasn't
Doedd Tom ddim		Tom wasn't
Doedden ni ddim	Don ni ddim	We weren't
Doeddech chi ddim	Doch chi ddim	You weren't
Doedden nhw ddim	Don nhw ddim	They weren't

For example:

Doedd hi ddim yn siopa yn Llundain	She wasn't shopping in London
Doeddech chi ddim yn gweithio'n galed	You weren't working hard
Doeddwn i ddim yn byw yn Llandudno	I wasn't living in Llandudno
Doedd y plant ddim yn y gwely	The children weren't in bed

● Remember that in negative sentences the linking **yn** comes after **ddim**

● Notice that the singular form of the verb is used with all nouns even with plural nouns:

Doedd y mynyddoedd ddim yn uchel	The mountains weren't high

● **Question and Answer forms**

Standard forms	Spoken forms	English	Yes/No
Oeddwn i?	On i?	Was I?	(Nac) Oeddet/ Oeddech
Oeddet ti?	Ot ti?	Were you?	(Nac) Oeddwn
Oedd e? (S.W.) Oedd o? (N.W.)		Was he?	(Nac) Oedd
Oedd hi?		Was she?	(Nac) Oedd
Oedd Tom?		Was Tom?	(Nac) Oedd
Oedden ni?	On ni?	Were we?	(Nac) Oedden
Oeddech chi?	Och chi?	Were you?	(Nac) Oeddech
Oedden nhw?	On nhw?	Were they?	(Nac) Oedden

For example:

Oedd hi'n siopa yn Llundain?	Was she shopping in London?
Oedd	Yes (she was)
Oeddech chi'n gweithio'n galed?	Were you working hard?
Nac oeddwn	No (I wasn't)
Oeddwn i'n rhy hwyr?	Was I too late? Yes (you were)
Oeddet/Oeddech	

● **Indefinite forms**

Unlike the present tense where definite and indefinite forms are distinguished by the use of **ydy** and **oes** respectively, no different form is required in the Imperfect Tense:

Roedd hi'n braf	It was fine
Roedd problem (S.W.)	There was a problem
Roedd 'na broblem (N.W.)	
Oedd John yno?	Was John there?
Oedd llawer yno? (S.W.)	Were there many there?
Oedd 'na lawer yno? (N.W.)	
Oedd/Nac oedd	Yes/No
Doedd yr ateb ddim yn iawn	The answer wasn't right
Doedd dim ateb (S.W.)	There was no answer
Doedd 'na ddim ateb (N.W.)	

3.5.3 Perfect Tense

Once again the forms of the Present Tense of the verb to be are used with all verb-nouns, but this time the linking word is **wedi** (i.e. wedi takes the place of **yn**, therefore the linking words **yn** and **wedi** cannot appear in the same sentence). Again, there is no mutation after **wedi**.

● **Affirmative forms**

Standard forms	Spoken forms	English
Rydw i wedi	Dw i 'di	I have
Rwyt ti wedi	Ti 'di	You have
Mae e wedi (S.W.) Mae o wedi (N.W.)	Mae e 'di (S.W.) Mae o 'di (N.W.)	He has
Mae hi wedi	Mae hi 'di	She has
Mae Tom wedi	Mae Tom 'di	Tom has
Rydyn ni wedi	'Dyn ni 'di (S.W.)/ 'Dan ni 'di (N.W.)	We have
Rydych chi wedi	'Dych chi 'di (S.W.)/ 'Dach chi 'di (N.W.)	You have
Maen nhw wedi	Maen nhw 'di	They have

For example:

Dw i wedi byw yn Llandudno   I have lived in Llandudno
'Dych chi wedi gweithio'n galed   You have worked hard
Mae hi wedi siopa yn Llundain   She has shopped in London

● **Negative forms**

Standard forms	Spoken forms	English
Dydw i ddim wedi	Dw i ddim 'di	I haven't
Dwyt ti ddim wedi	Ti ddim 'di	You haven't
Dydy e ddim wedi (S.W.)/ Dydy o ddim wedi (N.W.)	'Dyw e ddim 'di (S.W.)/ 'Dy o ddim 'di (N.W.)	He hasn't
Dydy hi ddim wedi	'Dyw hi ddim 'di (S.W.)/ 'Dy hi ddim 'di (N.W.)	She hasn't
Dydy Tom ddim wedi	'Dyw Tom ddim 'di (S.W.)/ 'Dy Tom ddim 'di (N.W.)	Tom hasn't
Dydyn ni ddim wedi	'Dyn ni ddim 'di (S.W.)/ 'Dan ni ddim 'di (N.W.)	We haven't
Dydych chi ddim wedi	'Dych chi ddim 'di(S.W.)/ 'Dach chi ddim 'di (N.W.)	You haven't
Dydyn nhw ddim wedi	'Dyn nhw ddim 'di (S.W.)/ 'Dan nhw ddim 'di (N.W.)	They haven't

For example:

Dydy hi ddim wedi siopa yn Llundain	She hasn't shopped in London
'Dych chi ddim wedi gweithio'n galed	You haven't worked hard
Dw i ddim wedi byw yn Llandudno	I have not lived in Llandudno

● **Question and Answer forms**

Standard forms	Spoken forms	English	Answer
Ydw i wedi?	'Dw i 'di?	Have I?	(Nac) Wyt/ Ydych
Wyt ti wedi?	Ti 'di?	Have you?	(Nac) Ydw
Ydy e wedi (S.W.)/ Ydy o wedi (N.W.)?	Ydy e 'di? Ydy o 'di?	Has he?	(Nac) Ydy
Ydy hi wedi?	Ydy hi 'di?	Has she?	(Nac) Ydy
Ydy Tom wedi?	Ydy Tom 'di?	Has Tom?	(Nac) Ydy
Ydyn ni wedi?	'Dyn ni 'di? (S.W.)/ 'Dan ni 'di? (N.W.)	Have we?	(Nac) Ydyn
Ydych chi wedi?	'Dych chi'di ? (S.W.)/ 'Dach chi 'di? (N.W.)	Have you?	(Nac) Ydych
Ydyn nhw wedi?	'Dyn nhw 'di? (S.W.)/ 'Dan nhw 'di? (N.W.)	Have they?	(Nac) Ydyn

● You'll will notice that the Yes/No replies are the same as for the Present Tense. In North Wales also people will reply to all persons of the verb by using:

Do	Yes
Naddo	No

For example:

Ydy hi wedi siopa yn Llundain?	Has she shopped in London?
Ydy/Do	Yes (she has)
Ydych chi wedi gweithio'n galed?	Have you worked hard?
Nac ydw/Naddo	No (I haven't)
Ydw i wedi byw yn Llandudno?	Have I lived in Llandudno?
Wyt/Ydych/Do	Yes (you have)

3.5.4 Pluperfect Tense

This is the farthest back in time that we can go. In this tense we use the Imperfect Tense forms of the verb 'to be' together with the linking word **wedi**. Again, remember that the linking words **yn** and **wedi** cannot be used in the same sentence.

● **Affirmative forms**

Standard forms	Spoken forms	English
Roeddwn i wedi	Ron i 'di	I had
Roeddet ti wedi	Rot ti 'di	You had
Roedd e wedi (S.W.) Roedd o wedi (N.W.)	Roedd e 'di Roedd o 'di	He had
Roedd hi wedi	Roedd hi 'di	She had
Roedd Tom wedi	Roedd Tom 'di	Tom had
Roedden ni wedi	Ron ni 'di	We had
Roeddech chi wedi	Roch chi 'di	You had
Roedden nhw wedi	Ron nhw 'di	They had

For example:

Roeddwn i wedi byw yn Llandudno	I had lived in Llandudno
Roeddech chi wedi gweithio'n galed	You had worked hard
Roedd hi wedi siopa yn Llundain	She had shopped in London

● Negative forms

Standard forms	Spoken forms	English
Doeddwn i ddim wedi	Don i ddim 'di	I hadn't
Doeddet ti ddim wedi	Dot ti ddim 'di	You hadn't
Doedd e ddim wedi (S.W.)/ Doedd o ddim wedi (N.W.)	Doedd e ddim 'di Doedd o ddim 'di	He hadn't
Doedd hi ddim wedi	Doedd hi ddim 'di	She hadn't
Doedd Tom ddim wedi	Doedd Tom ddim 'di	Tom hadn't
Doedden ni ddim wedi	Don ni ddim 'di	We hadn't
Doeddech chi ddim wedi	Doch chi ddim 'di	You hadn't
Doedden nhw ddim wedi	Don nhw ddim 'di	They hadn't

For example:

Doedd hi ddim wedi siopa yn Llundain	She hadn't shopped in London
Doeddech chi ddim wedi gweithio'n galed	You hadn't worked hard
Doeddwn i ddim wedi byw yn Llandudno	I hadn't lived in Llandudno

● Question and Answer forms

Standard forms	Spoken forms	English	Yes/No
Oeddwn i wedi?	On i 'di?	Had I?	(Nac) Oeddet/ Oeddech
Oeddet ti wedi?	Ot ti 'di?	Had you?	(Nac) Oeddwn
Oedd e wedi? (S.W.) Oedd o wedi? (N.W.)	Oedd e 'di? Oedd o 'di?	Had he	(Nac) Oedd
Oedd hi wedi?	Oedd hi 'di?	Had she	(Nac) Oedd
Oedd Tom wedi?	Oedd Tom 'di?	Had Tom	(Nac) Oedd
Oedden ni wedi?	On ni 'di?	Had we?	(Nac) Oedden
Oeddech chi wedi?	Och chi 'di?	Had you?	(Nac) Oeddech
Oedden nhw wedi?	On nhw 'di?	Had they?	(Nac) Oedden

For example:

Oedd hi wedi siopa yn Llundain? Oedd	Had she shopped in London? Yes (she had)
Oeddech chi wedi gweithio'n galed? Nac oeddwn	Had you worked hard? No (I hadn't)
Oeddwn i wedi byw yn Llandudno? Oeddet/Oeddech	Had I lived in Llandudno? Yes (you had)

3.5.5 Future Tense

In this tense (where a person will be doing something) we use the future forms of the verb 'to be' with all the verb-nouns joined by the linking **yn**.

● **Affirmative forms**

Standard forms	English
Fe/Mi fydda i	I will/shall be
Fe/Mi fyddi di	You will/shall be
Fe/Mi fydd e/o	He will/shall be
Fe/Mi fydd hi	She will/shall be
Fe/Mi fydd Tom	Tom will/shall be
Fe/Mi fyddwn ni	We will/shall be
Fe/Mi fyddwch chi	You will/shall be
Fe/Mi fyddan nhw	They will/shall be

● The verb forms begin with the consonant **b**:

Bydda i	Byddwn ni
Byddi di	Byddwch chi
Bydd Tom	Byddan nhw

These forms are rather literary and are often found in narrative but in ordinary speech, we tend to place the particles:

Mi	North Wales
Fe	South Wales

in front of the verb forms. These words have no translatable value but they have something to do with the rhythm of the language (much like a leading note in music – a note which leads in to the beat!). They cause the verb forms to undergo a Soft Mutation:

Mi fydda in byw yn Llandudno y flwyddyn nesa	I shall be living in Llandudno next year
Fe fyddwch chi'n gweithio'n galed	You'll be working hard
Mi/Fe fydd hi'n siopa yn Llundain	She'll be shopping in London

● **Negative forms**

Standard forms	English
Fydda i ddim	I won't/shall not be
Fyddi di ddim	You won't/shall not be
Fydd e/o ddim	He won't/shall not be
Fydd hi ddim	She won't/shall not be
Fydd Tom ddim	Tom won't/shall not be
Fyddwn ni ddim	We won't/shall not be
Fyddwch chi ddim	You won't/shall not be
Fyddan nhw ddim	They won't/shall not be

● As **Mi/Fe** are particles which denote the affirmative, they are not used in the negative:

Fydd hi ddim yn siopa yn Llundain	She won't be shopping in London
Fyddwch chi ddim yn gweithio'n galed	You won't be working hard
Fydda i ddim yn byw yn Llandudno	I won't be living in Llandudno

● **Question and Answer forms**

Standard forms	English	Yes
Fydda i?	Will I be?	Byddi
Fyddi di?	Will you be?	Bydda
Fydd e/o?	Will he be?	Bydd
Fydd hi?	Will she be?	Bydd
Fydd Tom?	Will Tom be?	Bydd
Fyddwn ni?	Will we be?	Byddwn
Fyddwch chi?	Will you be?	Byddwch
Fyddan nhw?	Will they be?	Byddan

● As **Mi/Fe** are particles which denote the affirmative, they are not used in the question forms.

● The negative reply 'No' is formed by placing **Na** in front of the Yes replies (note that it causes a Soft Mutation):

Na fydda	No (I won't be)
Na fyddan	No (they won't be)
Na fyddi	No (you won't be)

For example:

Fydd hi'n siopa yn Llundain?	Will she be shopping in London?
Na fydd	No
Fyddwch chi'n gweithio'n galed?	Will you be working hard?
Na fydda	No
Fydda i'n byw yn Llandudno?	Will I be living in Llandudno?
Na fyddi/Na fyddwch	No

● Indefinite forms

As with the Imperfect Tense, the third person singular is also used for indefinite forms:

Fe fydd lle (S.W.)	There will be room
Mi fydd 'na le (N.W.)	
Fydd lle? (S.W.)	Will there be room?
Fydd 'na le? (N.W.)	
Fydd dim lle (S.W.)	There won't be room
Fydd 'na ddim lle (N.W.)	

3.6 Verbs (short forms)

All the verb tenses in this section so far are called long forms because they are made up of the verb 'to be' forms linked by either **yn** or **wedi** to the verb-nouns.
The next two tenses – Past and Future – are called short forms because they are formed by adding endings to the stem of the verbs.

3.6.1 Past Tense

● Affirmative forms
These are the endings that are added to the stem of all regular verbs:

Standard form	Spoken form
-ais i	-es i
-aist ti	-est ti
-odd e/o	
-odd hi	
-odd Tom	
-on ni	
-och chi	
-on nhw	

● The stem of most verbs is found by dropping the final syllable of the verb-noun:

cerdded	(to walk)	cerdd
bwyta	(to eat)	bwyt
prynu	(to buy)	pryn
dysgu	(to learn)	dysg
canu	(to sing)	can

● Sometimes it is only the final letter which is dropped:

gweld	(to see)	gwel

● The stem of a few verbs consists of the whole verb-noun:

eistedd	(to sit)	eistedd
siarad	(to talk/speak)	siarad
edrych	(to look)	edrych
darllen	(to read)	darllen

● Some stems are irregular:

dweud	(to say)	dwed
cyrraedd	(to arrive)	cyrhaedd
aros	(to stop/wait)	arhos
gwrando	(to listen)	gwrandaw
gadael	(to leave)	gadaw
cymryd	(to take)	cymer
meddwl	(to think)	meddyli

● Here is an example of the Past Tense formed using the verb dysgu (to learn):

Dysgais (es) i	I learnt
Dysgaist (est) ti	You (familiar) learnt
Dysgodd e/o	He learnt
Dysgodd hi	She learnt
Dysgodd Tom	Tom learnt
Dysgon ni	We learnt
Dysgoch chi	You learnt
Dysgon nhw	They learnt

- Singular form of the verb is used with all nouns – even with plural nouns:

Dysgodd y plant	The children learnt

As with the Future Tense, in normal speech, we place **Mi/Fe** in front of these verb forms – with the Soft Mutation as before:

Fe/Mi ddysgais (es) i
Fe/Mi ddysgodd Tom
Fe/Mi ddysgon ni

For example:

Mi ddarllenodd Tom y papur yn y gwely	Tom read the paper in bed
Fe welodd hi'r ffilm neithiwr	She saw the film last night
Fe brynais i ffrog newydd ddoe	I bought a new dress yesterday

- ### Negative forms

Drop the positive or affirmative participle Mi/Fe but keep the Soft Mutation at the beginning of the verb forms – except those verbs which begin with **c**, **p** or **t** (which undergo an Aspirate Mutation):

Fe/Mi ddysgais (es) i	Ddysgais (es) i ddim
Fe/Mi ddysgaist (est) ti	Ddysgaist (est) ti ddim
Fe/Mi ddysgodd e/o	Ddysgodd e/o ddim
Fe/Mi ddysgodd hi	Ddysgodd hi ddim
Fe/Mi ddysgodd Tom	Ddysgodd Tom ddim
Fe/Mi ddysgon ni	Ddysgon ni ddim
Fe/Mi ddysgoch chi	Ddysgoch chi ddim
Fe/Mi ddysgon nhw	Ddysgon nhw ddim

For example:

Ddarllenodd Tom ddim papur yn y gwely	Tom didn't read a paper in bed
Welodd hi ddim ffilm neithiwr	She didn't see a film last night
Wisgais i ddim ffrog newydd ddoe	I didn't wear a new dress yesterday

● As stated above, verbs which begin with **c**, **p** or **t** begin with an Aspirate Mutation in the Negative Past Tense forms. For example, **cysgu – to sleep**

Fe/Mi gysgais (es) i	Chysgais (es) i ddim
Fe/Mi gysgaist (est) ti	Chysgaist (est) ti ddim
Fe/Mi gysgodd e/o	Chysgodd e/o ddim
Fe/Mi gysgodd hi	Chysgodd hi ddim
Fe/Mi gysgodd Tom	Chysgodd Tom ddim
Fe/Mi gysgon ni	Chysgon ni ddim
Fe/Mi gysgoch chi	Chysgoch chi ddim
Fe/Mi gysgon nhw	Chysgon nhw ddim

● **Question and Answer forms**

Merely drop the positive marker **Mi/Fe**, keep the Soft Mutation and adopt a questioning tone of voice.

● The replies in this tense are the same in all persons:

Yes	Do
No	Naddo

Ddysgais (es) i?	Did I learn?	Do/Naddo
Ddysgaist (est) ti	Did you learn?	Do/Naddo
Ddysgodd e/o?	Did he learn?	Do/Naddo
Ddysgodd hi?	Did she learn?	Do/Naddo
Ddysgodd Tom?	Did Tom learn?	Do/Naddo
Ddysgon ni?	Did we learn?	Do/Naddo
Ddysgoch chi?	Did you learn?	Do/Naddo
Ddysgon nhw?	Did they learn?	Do/Naddo

For example:

Ddarllenodd Tom y papur yn y gwely? Do	Did Tom read the paper in bed? Yes
Welodd hi ffilm neithiwr? Naddo	Did she see a film last night? No
Wisgaist ti ffrog newydd ddoe? Do	Did you wear a new dress yesterday? Yes

3.6.2 Past Tense (irregular verbs)

The five main irregular verbs in Welsh are:

mynd	to go
dod	to come
gwneud	to do/make
cael	to have/receive
bod	to be

● **Affirmative forms**

The first three form a group of their own as they follow a similar pattern:

mynd		dod		gwneud	
South Wales	**North Wales**	**South Wales**	**North Wales**	**South Wales**	**North Wales**
Fe es i	Mi es i	Fe ddes i	Mi ddois	Fe wnes i	Mi wnes i
Fe est ti	Mi est ti	Fe ddest ti	Mi ddoist ti	Fe wnest ti	Mi wnest ti
Fe aeth e	Mi aeth o	Fe ddaeth e	Mi ddôth o	Fe wnaeth e	Mi wnaeth o
Fe aeth hi	Mi aeth hi	Fe ddaeth hi	Mi ddôth hi	Fe wnaeth hi	Mi wnaeth hi
Fe aeth Tom	Mi aeth Tom	Fe ddaeth Tom	Mi ddôth Tom	Fe wnaeth Tom	Mi wnaeth Tom
Fe aethon ni	Mi aethon ni	Fe ddaethon ni	Mi ddaethon ni	Fe wnaethon ni	Mi wnaethon ni
Fe aethoch chi	Mi aethoch chi	Fe ddaethoch chi	Mi ddaethoch chi	Fe wnaethoch chi	Mi wnaethoch chi
Fe aethon nhw	Mi aethon nhw	Fe ddaethon nhw	Mi ddaethon nhw	Fe wnaethon nhw	Mi wnaethon nhw

For example:

Fe aeth y plant i'r ysgol ar y bws	The children went to school on the bus
Mi aethon nhw i chwarae yn y parc ar ôl yr ysgol	They went to play in the park after school
Mi es i i'r gwely'n gynnar neithiwr	I went to bed early last night
Fe ddaeth Mair adre ddoe	Mair came home yesterday
Fe ddaethon ni i'r parti mewn tacsi	We came to the party in a taxi
Fe ddest ti i'r gwaith gyda Bill y bore 'ma	You came to work with Bill this morning
Mi wnaethon nhw'r gwaith ddydd Sadwrn	They did the work on Saturday
Fe wnaeth hi gacen i de	She made a cake for tea
Mi wnaethon ni sŵn	We made a noise

● The Past Tense of **cael** (to have) needs to be learnt separately:

Fe ges i	Fe gawson ni
Fe gest ti	Fe gawsoch chi
Fe gafodd e/Fe gafodd o	Fe gawson nhw
Fe gafodd hi	
Fe gafodd Tom	

For example:

Mi ges i gar newydd y llynedd	I had a new car last year
Fe gawson nhw salad i swper	They had salad for supper

● In North Wales, in the spoken language, **cael** also follows the pattern of the other three irregular verbs:

Mi ges i	Mi gaethon ni
Mi gest ti	Mi gaethoch chi
Mi gaeth o	Mi gaethon nhw
Mi gaeth hi	
Mi gaeth Tom	

For example:

Mi gaethon ni dost i frecwast	We had toast for breakfast
Mi gaeth Beti wobr yn yr eisteddfod	Beti had a prize at the eisteddfod

- Notice that the singular form of the verb is used with all nouns even with plural nouns:

> Fe gafodd y llewod fwyd am ddau o'r gloch   The lions had food at two o'clock

- ### Negative forms

Negatives are formed in exactly the same way as regular verbs. Drop the positive marker **Mi/Fe**, keep the Soft Mutation (except for **cael** which undertakes an Aspirate Mutation) and add **ddim**:

> Fe/Mi aeth hi   Aeth hi ddim
> Fe/Mi ddaethon nhw   Ddaethon nhw ddim
> Fe/Mi wnest ti   Wnest ti ddim
> Fe/Mi ges i   Ches i ddim

- ### Question and Answer forms

Questions are formed in exactly the same way as regular verbs. Drop the positive marker **Mi/Fe** and keep the Soft Mutation:

> Fe/Mi aeth hi   Aeth hi?   Do/Naddo
> Fe/Mi ddaethon nhw   Ddaethon nhw?   Do/Naddo
> Fe/Mi wnaeth y plant   Wnaeth y plant?   Do/Naddo
> Fe/Mi fuon ni   Fuon ni?   Do/Naddo
> Fe/Mi gest ti   Gest ti?   Do/Naddo

3.6.3 Past Tense - Bod (to be)

The exact meaning of the Past Tense of **bod** (to be) is difficult to convey as it doesn't exist in English. So we have to translate it by using 'went' or 'have been' or 'was/were'. Here are the forms:

> Fe/Mi fues i   Fe/Mi fuon ni
> Fe/Mi fuest ti   Fe/Mi fuoch chi
> Fe/Mi fuodd e/o   Fe/Mi fuon nhw
> Fe/Mi fuodd hi
> Fe/Mi fuodd Tom

For example:

Fe fues i yng Nghaerdydd ddoe	I went to/have been in/ was in Cardiff yesterday
Mi fuon nhw i Sbaen ym mis Awst	They went to/have been to/ were in Spain in August
Mi fuodd Ann mewn parti nos Sadwrn	Ann went to/has been to/ was in a party on Saturday night

● The **bues** forms can also be used with another verb. The exact meaning in English is quite difficult to convey:

Mi fuon ni'n siopa ddoe	We went shopping/ have been shopping yesterday
Fe fues i'n chwarae tennis ar ôl cinio ddydd Sadwrn	I was playing/went playing tennis after lunch on Saturday

Negative forms

● Negatives are formed in exactly the same way as regular verbs. Drop the positive marker **Mi/Fe**, keep the Soft Mutation and add **ddim**:

Fe/Mi fuodd hi	Fuodd hi ddim
Fe/Mi fuon nhw	Fuon nhw ddim
Fe/Mi fuest ti	Fuest ti ddim

● **Question and Answer forms**

Questions are formed in exactly the same way as regular verbs. Drop the positive marker **Mi/Fe** and keep the Soft Mutation:

Fe/Mi fuodd hi	Fuodd hi?	Do/Naddo
Fe/Mi fuon nhw	Fuon nhw?	Do/Naddo
Fe/Mi fuon ni	Fuon ni?	Do/Naddo

3.6.4 Past Tense (alternative short forms)

There is an alternative method of forming the short Past Tense for all verbs, regular and irregular. Instead of adding endings to the stem of each verb (as seen above), it is possible to use any verb-noun with the Past Tense forms of **gwneud**, or in North Wales **ddaru**, remembering that the verb-noun will undergo a Soft Mutation.

● **Affirmative forms**

Fe/Mi wnes i ddysgu'r gwaith	I learnt the work
Fe/Mi wnest ti brynu car newydd eleni	You bought a new car this year
Fe/Mi wnaeth Tom ddod adre'n gynnar heddiw	Tom came home early today
Fe/Mi wnaethon ni fynd i'r parti	We went to the party
Fe/Mi wnaethoch chi dalu'r bil	You paid the bill
Fe/Mi wnaethon nhw gofio'r gwaith	They remembered the work

● **Negative forms**

Notice that the mutation after the verb now happens to the word **dim** which becomes **ddim** so the word which follows it does not need to be mutated in these negative sentences:

Wnes i ddim dysgu'r gwaith	I didn't learn the work
Wnest ti ddim prynu car newydd eleni	You didn't buy a new car this year
Wnaeth Tom ddim dod adre'n gynnar heddiw	Tom didn't come home early today
Wnaethon ni ddim mynd i'r parti	We didn't go to the party
Wnaethoch chi ddim talu'r bil	You didn't pay the bill
Wnaethon nhw ddim cofio'r gwaith	They didn't remember the work

● **Question and Answer forms**

Wnes i ddysgu'r gwaith? Naddo	Did I learn the work? No
Wnest ti brynu car newydd eleni? Do	Did you buy a new car this year? Yes
Wnaeth Tom ddod adre'n gynnar heddiw? Naddo	Did Tom come home early today? No
Wnaethon ni fynd i'r parti? Do	Did we go to the party? Yes
Wnaethoch chi dalu'r bil? Naddo	Did you pay the bill? No
Wnaethon nhw gofio'r gwaith? Do	Did they remember the work? Yes

● **Ddaru** is used with every person, and with statements, questions and negative sentences:

Ddaru mi ddysgu'r gwaith	I learnt the work
Ddaru ti ddim prynu car newydd eleni	You didn't buy a new car this year
Ddaru ni fynd i'r parti? Do/Naddo	Did we go to the party? Yes/No

3.6.5 Future Tense

This tense again is formed by adding endings to the stem of all regular verbs. This gives the meaning of someone will do something rather than someone will be doing something (as in the long form).

● **Affirmative forms**

These are the endings that are added to the stem of all regular verbs.

-a i	-an ni
-i di	-wch chi
-iff e/hi/Tom (S.W.)	-an nhw
-ith o/hi/Tom (N.W.)	

● In the 3rd person singular, the ending in North Wales is **-ith** whilst in South Wales it is **-iff**.

Here are some examples using **dysgu** – to learn:

Dysga i	I'll learn
Dysgi di	You'll learn
Dysgiff e (S.W.)	He'll learn
Dysgith o (N.W.)	He'll learn
Dysgiff/ith hi	She'll learn
Dysgiff/ith Tom	Tom will learn
Dysgwn ni	We'll learn
Dysgwch chi	You'll learn
Dysgiff/ith y plant	The children will learn
Dysgan nhw	They'll learn

● Notice that the singular form of the verb is used with all nouns even with plural nouns

● As mentioned above, in normal speech, we place **Mi/Fe** in front of these verb forms – with the Soft Mutation as before:

Fe/Mi ddysga i	Fe/Mi ddysgwn ni
Fe/ddysgi di	Fe/Mi ddysgwch chi
Fe ddysgiff e (S.W.)	Fe/Mi ddysgan nhw
Mi ddysgith o (N.W.)	
Fe/Mi ddysgiff/ith hi	
Fe/Mi ddysgiff/ith Tom	

● **Negative forms**

Drop the positive or affirmative marker **Mi/Fe** but keep the Soft Mutation at the beginning of the verb forms – except those verbs which begin with **c**, **p** or **t** (which undergo an Aspirate Mutation):

Fe/Mi ddysga i	Ddysga i ddim
Fe/Mi ddysgi di	Ddysgi di ddim
Fe/Mi ddysgiff e/hi (S.W.)	Ddysgiff e/hi ddim
Fe/Mi ddysgiff o/hi (N.W.)	Ddysgiff o/hi ddim
Fe/Mi ddysgiff/ith Tom	Ddysgiff/ith Tom ddim
Fe/Mi ddysgwn ni	Ddysgwn ni ddim
Fe/Mi ddysgwch chi	Ddysgwch chi ddim
Fe/Mi ddysgiff/ith y plant	Ddysgiff/ith y plant ddim
Fe/Mi ddysgan nhw	Ddysgan nhw ddim

For example:

Ddarlleniff/ith Tom ddim papur yn y gwely	Tom won't read a paper in bed
Weliff/ith hi ddim ffilm heno	She won't see a film tonight
Wisga i ddim ffrog newydd yfory	I won't wear a new dress tomorrow

● As stated above, verbs which begin with **c**, **p** or **t** begin with an Aspirate Mutation in the Negative Past Tense forms. For example, **cysgu – to sleep**:

Fe/Mi gysga i	Chysga i ddim
Fe/Mi gysgi di	Chysgi di ddim
Fe/Mi gysgwch chi	Chysgwch chi ddim
Fe/Mi gysgiff/ith e/o	Chysgiff/ith e/o ddim
Fe/Mi gysgiff/ith hi	Chysgiff/ith hi ddim
Fe/Mi gysgiff/ith Tom	Chysgiff/ith Tom ddim
Fe/Mi gysgwn ni	Chysgwn ni ddim
Fe/Mi gysgwch chi	Chysgwch chi ddim
Fe/Mi gysgiff/ith y plant	Chysgiff/ith y plant ddim
Fe/Mi gysgan nhw	Chysgan nhw ddim

● **Question and Answer forms**

Merely drop the positive marker **Mi/Fe**, keep the Soft Mutation and adopt a questioning tone of voice. The replies in this tense are based on the verb gwneud:

Ddysga i?	Will I learn?	Gwnei/Gwnewch
Ddysgi di?	Will you (familiar) learn?	Gwnaf (S.W.)/ Wna i (N.W.)
Ddysgiff e?	Will he learn?	Gwnaiff (S.W.)
Ddysgith o?	Will he learn?	Gwneith (N.W.)
Ddysgiff/ith hi?	Will she learn?	Gwnaiff (S.W.)/ Gwneith (N.W.)
Ddysgiff/ith Tom?	Will Tom learn?	Gwnaiff (S.W.)/ Gwneith (N.W.)
Ddysgwn ni?	Will we learn?	Gwnawn/Gwnewch
Ddysgwch chi?	Will you learn?	Gwnewch/Gwnawn
Ddysgan nhw?	Will they learn?	Gwnân

● The No replies are formed by placing **Na** in front of the Yes forms, which undergo a Soft Mutation:

Gwnaf	Yes (I will)	Gwnawn	Yes (we will)
Na wnaf	No (I won't)	Na wnawn	No (we won't)

For example:

Ddarlleniff Tom y papur yn y gwely?   Will Tom read the paper in bed?
Gwnaiff   Yes

Ddarllenith Tom y papur yn y gwely?   Will Tom read the paper in bed?
Gwneith   Yes

Welan nhw ffilm heno? Na wnân   Will they see a film tonight? No

Wisgi di ffrog newydd yfory?   Will you wear a new dress tomorrow?
Gwna   Yes

3.6.6 Future Tense (irregular verbs)

● The five main irregular verbs in Welsh are:

mynd	to go
gwneud	to do/make
cael	to have/receive
dod	to come
bod	to be

You have already seen the Future forms of the verb **bod** used to form the Future Tense (long form).

● **Affirmative forms**

The first three form a group of their own as they follow a similar pattern.

mynd	cael	gwneud
Fe/Mi af fi	Fe/Mi gaf fi	Fe/Mi wnaf fi
Fe/Mi ei di	Fe/Mi gei di	Fe/Mi wnei di
Fe aiff e/hi (S.W.)/ Mi eith o/hi (N.W.)	Fe gaiff e/hi (S.W.)/ Mi geith o/hi (N.W.)	Fe wnaiff e/hi (S.W.)/ Mi wneith o/hi (N.W.)
Fe aiff Tom (S.W.)/ Mi eith Tom (N.W.)	Fe gaiff Tom (S.W.)/ Mi geith Tom (N.W.)	Fe wnaiff Tom (S.W.)/ Mi wneith Tom (N.W.)
Fe/Mi awn ni	Fe/Mi gawn ni	Fe/Mi wnawn ni
Fe/Mi ewch chi	Fe/Mi gewch chi	Fe/Mi wnewch chi
Fe/Mi ân nhw	Fe/Mi gân nhw	Fe/Mi wnân nhw

The 1st person forms often drop the **f** in speech:

Fe/Mi â i	Fe/Mi ga i	Fe/Mi wna i

For example:

Fe aiff y plant i'r ysgol ar y bws	The children will go to school on the bus '
Mi ân nhw i chwarae yn y parc ar ôl yr ysgol	They'll go to play in the park after school
Fe/Mi af fi i'r gwely'n gynnar heno	I'll go to bed early tonight
Mi gaf fi gar newydd y flwyddyn nesa	I'll get a new car next year
Fe gaiff Beti wobr yn yr eisteddfod	Beti will get a prize at the eisteddfod
Mi gân nhw salad i swper	They'll have salad for supper
Mi wnân nhw'r gwaith ddydd Sadwrn	They'll do the work on Saturday
Fe wnaiff hi gacen i de	She'll make a cake for tea
Mi wnawn ni sŵn	We'll make a noise

● The Future Tense of **dod** is a little different:

Fe/Mi ddof fi	Fe/Mi ddown ni
Fe/Mi ddoi di	Fe/Mi ddewch chi
Fe/Mi ddaw e/o	Fe/Mi ddôn nhw
Fe/Mi ddaw hi	
Fe/Mi ddaw Tom	

● The 1st person form often drop the **f** in speech:

Fe/Mi ddo i

For example:

Mi ddaw Mair adre yfory	Mair will come home tomorrow
Fe ddown ni i'r parti mewn tacsi	We'll come to the party in a taxi
Fe ddoi di i'r gwaith gyda Bill	You'll come to work with Bill

● Negative forms

Negatives are formed in exactly the same way as regular verbs. Drop the positive marker **Mi/Fe**, keep the Soft Mutation (except for **cael** which undertakes an Aspirate Mutation) and add **ddim**:

Fe/Mi ân nhw	Ân nhw ddim
Fe/Mi ddaw hi	Ddaw hi ddim
Fe/Mi wnei di	Wnei di ddim
Fe/Mi fydd y plant	Fydd y plant ddim
Fe/Mi gawn ni	Chawn ni ddim

● Question and Answer forms

Questions are formed in exactly the same way as regular verbs. Drop the positive marker **Mi/Fe** and keep the Soft Mutation:

Fe/Mi ân nhw	Ân nhw?
Fe/Mi ddaw hi	Ddaw hi?
Fe/Mi wnei di	Wnei di?
Fe/Mi fydd y plant	Fydd y plant?
Fe/Mi gawn ni	Gawn ni?

● The unmutated forms of these five verbs are used to convey Yes/No

● The negative is formed in the usual way by placing **Na** in front of the affirmative forms. This causes a Soft Mutation with the **dod/gwneud/bod** forms, but an Aspirate Mutation with the **cael** forms.

For example:

Ân nhw i'r parti? Ân	Will they go to the party? Yes (they will go)
Ddaw hi adre'n gynnar o'r ysgol? Na ddaw	Will she come home early from school? No (she won't come)
Gawn ni gar newydd eleni? Na chawn	Will we have a new car this year? No (we won't have)

- Note that the future tense of **cael** is also used to ask for permission (May I? and May I have?):

Ga i fynd?	May I go?
Ga i ddiod?	May I have a drink?
Gei di aros?	May you stay?/
	Are you allowed to stay?
Gaiff John lifft? (S.W.)	May/Can John have a lifft?
Geith John lifft? (N.W.)	May/Can John have a lifft?

- The same rules as above apply, i.e. Aspirate Mutation in the negative:

Chewch chi ddim mynd	You may not go/
	You are not allowed to go

- The verb (in the appropriate person) is used to answer:

Ga i aros?	Can I stay?
Cewch	Yes (you may)
Na chewch	No (you may not)
Gân nhw ddiod?	May they have a drink?
Cân	Yes (they may)
Na chân	No (they may not)

- Note that the word immediately following the subject mutates, but that there is no mutation after ddim:

Ga i fynd?	Cha i ddim mynd

3.6.7 Future Tense (alternative short forms)

Instead of adding endings to the stem of each verb it's possible to use any verb-noun with the Future Tense forms of **gwneud**, remembering that the verb-noun will undergo a Soft Mutation.

● **Affirmative forms**

For example:

Fe/Mi wna i ddysgu'r gwaith	I'll learn the work
Fe/Mi wnei di brynu car newydd eleni	You'll buy a new car this year
Fe/Mi wnaiff/wneith Tom ddod adre'n gynnar heddiw	Tom will come home early today
Fe/Mi wnawn ni fynd i'r parti	We'll go to the party
Fe/Mi wnewch chi dalu'r bil	You'll pay the bill
Fe/Mi wnân nhw gofio'r gwaith	They'll remember the work

● **Negative forms**

Notice that the mutation after the verb now happens on the word **dim**, which becomes **ddim** so the word which follows it doesn't need to be mutated in these negative sentences:

Wna i ddim dysgu'r gwaith	I won't learn the work
Wnei di ddim prynu car newydd eleni	You won't buy a new car
Wnaiff/Wneith Tom ddim dod adre'n gynnar heddiw	Tom won't come home early today
Wnawn ni ddim mynd i'r parti	We won't go to the party
Wnewch chi ddim talu'r bil	You won't pay the bill
Wnân nhw ddim cofio'r gwaith	They won't remember the work

● **Question and Answer forms**

For example:

Wna i ddysgu'r gwaith?	Will I learn the work?
Gwnei/Gwnewch	Yes (you will)
Wnei di brynu car newydd eleni?	Will you buy a new car this year?
Na wnaf	No (I won't)
Wnaiff/Wneith Tom ddod adre'n gynnar heddiw? Gwnaiff/Gwneith	Will Tom come home early today? Yes (he will)
Wnawn ni fynd i'r parti? Na wnawn	Will we go to the party? No (we won't)
Wnewch chi dalu'r bil? Gwnawn/Gwnaf	Will you pay the bill? Yes (we will/I will)
Wnân nhw gofio'r gwaith? Gwnân	Will they remember the work? Yes (they will)

3.6.8 Conditional Tense

As mentioned above, the participles **Mi/Fe** are used in front of these forms in normal speech.

- **Affirmative forms**

Fe fyddwn i	Mi faswn i	I would
Fe fyddet ti	Mi faset ti	You would
Fe fyddai fe/fo	Mi fasai fe/fo	He would
Fe fyddai hi	Mi fasai hi	She would
Fe fyddai Tom	Mi fasai Tom	Tom would
Fe fydden ni	Mi fasen ni	We would
Fe fyddech chi	Mi fasech chi	You would
Fe fydden nhw	Mi fasen nhw	They would

These forms are again followed by the linking **yn** which causes no mutation.

- **Negative forms**

Fyddwn i ddim	Faswn i ddim	I wouldn't
Fyddet ti ddim	Faset ti ddim	You wouldn't
Fyddai fe/fo ddim	Fasai fe/fo ddim	He wouldn't
Fyddai hi ddim	Fasai hi ddim	She wouldn't
Fyddai Tom ddim	Fasai Tom ddim	Tom wouldn't
Fydden ni ddim	Fasen ni ddim	We wouldn't
Fyddech chi ddim	Fasech chi ddim	You wouldn't
Fydden nhw ddim	Fasen nhw ddim	They wouldn't

- **Question and Answer forms**

Fyddwn i?	Faswn i?	Byddet/Byddech/Baset/Basech
Fyddet ti ?	Faset ti?	Byddwn/Baswn
Fyddai fe/fo?	Fasai fe/fo?	Byddai/Basai
Fyddai hi?	Fasai hi?	Byddai/Basai
Fyddai Dilys?	Fasai Dilys?	Byddai/Basai
Fydden ni?	Fasen ni?	Bydden/Byddech/Basen/Basech
Fyddech chi?	Fasech chi?	Bydden/Basen
Fydden nhw?	Fasen nhw?	Bydden/Basen

These forms are again followed by the linking **yn** which causes no mutation.

● Negative replies are formed as usual by placing **Na** in front of the
Affirmative forms, not forgetting the Soft Mutation:

Byddwn/Baswn	Yes (I would)
Na fyddwn/Na faswn	No (I wouldn't)
Byddech/Basech	Yes (you would)
Na fyddech/Na fasech	No (you wouldn't)

For example:

Mi fasen ni'n bwyta sbageti yn yr Eidal	We would eat spaghetti in Italy
Faswn i ddim yn gwneud sŵn	I wouldn't make a noise
Fyddai'r plant yn cerdded i'r ysgol?	Would the children walk to school?
Bydden	Yes

The subordinate clause of a 'would' sentence, whether it comes at the
beginning or at the end of the sentence, usually begins with **if**. In English, the
verb which follows is often a Past Tense verb, but on further investigation it isn't
really the Past Tense that's required. Consider this sentence:

I would buy a new car, if I had enough money.

It means:
I would buy a new car, if I were to have enough money.
I would buy a new car, if I would have enough money.

In Welsh, this 'if' pattern uses the following:

Tawn i/Taswn i	If I were to (would)
Taet ti/Taset ti	If you were to (would)
Tai fe/Tasai fo	If he were to (would)
Tai hi/Tasai hi	If she were to (would)
Tai Dilys/Tasai Dilys	If Dilys were to (would)
Taen ni/Tasen ni	If we were to (would)
Taech chi/Tasech chi	If you were to (would)
Taen nhw/Tasen nhw	If they were to (would)

These forms are again followed by the linking **yn** which causes no mutation.

For example:

Fe/Mi faswn i'n gweld Twr Eiffel, taswn i'n mynd i Baris	I would see the Eiffel Tower, if I went (were to go/would go) to Paris
Taset ti'n mynd i'r parti, fe faswn i'n mynd hefyd	If you went (were to go/would go) to the party, I would go too
Tasen nhw'n gyfoethog, fe fasen nhw'n prynu cwch hwylio	If they were wealthy, they would buy a yacht

3.6.9 Would like (short forms)

● **Affirmative forms**

Fe/Mi hoffwn i	I would like
Fe/Mi hoffet ti	You would like (familiar)
Fe/Mi hoffai fe/fo	He would like
Fe/Mi hoffai hi	She would like
Fe/Mi hoffai Tom	Tom would like
Fe/Mi hoffen ni	We would like
Fe/Mi hoffech chi	You would like
Fe/Mi hoffen nhw	They would like

There is no linking **yn** after these forms and the verb-nouns/nouns which follow these short affirmative forms undergo a Soft Mutation.

● **Negative forms**

Hoffwn i ddim	I wouldn't like
Hoffet ti ddim	You wouldn't like
Hoffai fe/fo ddim	He wouldn't like
Hoffai hi ddim	She wouldn't like
Hoffai Dilys ddim	Dilys wouldn't like
Hoffen ni ddim	We wouldn't like
Hoffech chi ddim	You wouldn't like
Hoffen nhw ddim	They wouldn't like

There is no linking **yn** after these forms and there is no mutation in the verb-nouns/nouns which follow these short negative forms.

● Question and Answer forms

Hoffwn i?	Would I like?	(Na) hoffet/hoffech
Hoffet ti?	Would you like?	(Na) hoffwn
Hoffai fe/fo?	Would he like?	(Na) hoffai
Hoffai hi?	Would she like?	(Na) hoffai
Hoffai Dilys?	Would Dilys like?	(Na) hoffai
Hoffen ni?	Would we like?	(Na) hoffen/hoffech
Hoffech chi?	Would you like?	(Na) hoffen
Hoffen nhw?	Would they like?	(Na) hoffen

There is no linking **yn** after these forms and the verb-nouns/nouns which follow these short question forms undergo a Soft Mutation:

Fe/Mi hoffai'r plant fynd i weld Mickey Mouse	The children would like to go to see Mickey Mouse
Hoffen ni ddim bwyta malwod	We wouldn't like to eat snails
Hoffet ti gael porc i ginio? Hoffwn	Would you like to have pork for dinner? Yes (I would)

3.6.10 Ought to/Should

● Affirmative forms

Fe/Mi ddylwn i	I ought to/should
Fe/Mi ddylet ti	You ought to/should
Fe/Mi ddylai fe/fo	He ought to/should
Fe/Mi ddylai hi	She ought to/should
Fe/Mi ddylai Tom	Tom ought to/should
Fe/Mi ddylen ni	We ought to/should
Fe/Mi ddylech chi	You ought to/should
Fe/Mi ddylen nhw	They ought to/should

Notice that there is no linking **yn** after this pattern and the verb-noun/noun which follows the affirmative forms undergoes a Soft Mutation.

● **Negative forms**

Ddylwn i ddim	I shouldn't
Ddylet ti ddim	You shouldn't
Ddylai fe/fo ddim	He shouldn't
Ddylai hi ddim	She shouldn't
Ddylai Tom ddim	Tom shouldn't
Ddylen ni ddim	We shouldn't
Ddylech chi ddim	You shouldn't
Ddylen nhw ddim	They shouldn't

Notice that there is no linking **yn** after this pattern and the verb-noun follows immediately without a mutation.

● **Question and Answer forms**

Ddylwn i?	Should I?	Na ddylet/Na ddylech
Ddylet ti?	Should you?	Na ddylwn
Ddylai fe/fo?	Should he?	Na ddylai
Ddylai hi?	Should she?	Na ddylai
Ddylai Dilys?	Should Dilys?	Na ddylai
Ddylen ni?	Should we?	Na ddylen/Na ddylech
Ddylech chi?	Should you?	Na ddylen
Ddylen nhw?	Should they?	Na ddylen

The verb-noun/noun following the question form undergoes a Soft Mutation. As usual the negative reply is formed by placing **Na** in front of the affirmative forms, remembering the Soft Mutation:

Dylwn	Yes (I should)
Na ddylwn	No (I shouldn't)
Dylet	Yes (you should)
Na ddylet	No (you shouldn't)

For example:

Fe/Mi ddylai'r plant fynd i'r gwely'n gynnar heno	The children ought to go to bed early tonight
Ddylen ni ddim yfed gormod o alcohol	We shouldn't drink too much alcohol
Ddylet ti gael salad i ginio?	Should you have salad for dinner?
Dylwn	Yes (I should)

3.6.11 Must/Have to

● **Affirmative forms**

(Mae) rhaid i mi/fi	I must/have to
(Mae) rhaid i ti	You must/have to
(Mae) rhaid iddo fe (S.W.)	He must/has to
(Mae) rhaid iddo fo (N.W.)	He must/has to
(Mae) rhaid iddi hi	She must/has to
(Mae) rhaid i Tom	Tom must/has to
(Mae) rhaid i ni	We must/have to
(Mae) rhaid i chi	You must/have to
(Mae) rhaid iddyn nhw	They must/have to

Mae is in brackets to show that it is often omitted in everyday speech.

● **Negative forms**

To make a negative statement, change **Mae** to **Does dim**:

Does dim rhaid i ni	We don't have to
Does dim rhaid iddi hi	She doesn't have to

● **Question forms**

To ask a question, change **Mae** to **Oes?**

Oes rhaid i chi?	Must you/Do you have to?
Oes rhaid iddyn nhw?	Must they/Do they have to?

- In the Past Tense use the Imperfect (**Roedd**, **Oedd?** and **Doedd dim**):

Roedd rhaid i mi/fi	I had to
Roedd rhaid iddo fo (N.W.)	He had to
Oedd rhaid i ti?	Did you have to?
Oedd rhaid iddyn nhw?	Did they have to?
Doedd dim rhaid i chi	You didn't have to
Doedd dim rhaid i ni	We didn't have to

- The verb-noun which follows the full **rhaid** (must) pattern undergoes a Soft Mutation. We often omit **Mae** in everyday speech:

(Mae) rhaid iddyn nhw ddysgu Cymraeg	They must learn Welsh
Oes rhaid i ti fynd adre?	Must you/Do you have to go home?

- You will notice that the initial verb form which is used with **rhaid** is always in the 3rd person singular. This is true of all tenses:

```
Mae rhaid i ............
Roedd rhaid i .............
Fe/Mi fydd rhaid i ...............
Tasai rhaid i .................
Fe/Mi fasai rhaid i ..................
```

The full pattern doesn't have to be used. It's possible to make an impersonal statement by placing a verb-noun immediately after **rhaid** thus avoiding the mutation:

(Mae) rhaid mynd i'r gwely'n gynnar heno	One (i.e. I/We) must go to bed early tonight
(Mae) rhaid gweld John	One (i.e. I/We) must see John

3.6.12 Prepositions which follow certain verbs

It is important to learn some verbs with the prepositions that follow them because these can vary from language to language. This is arguably the most difficult element in any language as there is often no logical explanation for the use of a particular preposition after a certain verb. This is true of a number of languages, including English. Consider the following: fill in, fill out, fill up; work out; cut up; drink up; listen to; listen for; think of; think up; round up; round on; bring about; bring in; bring on; bring up.

Here are some examples in Welsh:

edrych ar	to look at
gwrando ar	to listen to
siarad efo (N.W.)	to talk/speak to
siarad â (S.W.)	to talk/speak to
cwrdd â	to meet
dweud wrth	to tell
gweithio i	to work for
gofyn i	to ask (someone)
rhoi i	to give to
edrych ymlaen at	to look forward to
cofio at	to remember to
anfon at	to send to (a person)

Remember that these prepositions have personal forms they conjugate – these are dealt with in 3.4:

Dw i'n hoffi edrych arno fe/fo	I like looking at him
Wyt ti wedi ysgrifennu ati hi?	Have you written to her?

3.6.13 Commands

● **Regular verbs**

Most verbs fall into this group. Endings are added to the stem of the verb
(this is covered in 3.6.1). The polite/formal singular and plural command
ending is **–wch**:

cerdded (to walk)	cerddwch!
bwyta (to eat)	bwytwch!
prynu (to buy)	prynwch!
dysgu (to learn)	dysgwch!
canu (to sing)	canwch!
eistedd (to sit)	eisteddwch!
siarad (to talk/speak)	siaradwch!
edrych (to look)	edrychwch!
darllen (to read)	darllenwch!
dweud (to say)	dwedwch!

● The familiar singular command ending is **–a**:

cerdded (to walk)	cerdda!
bwyta (to eat)	bwyta!
prynu (to buy)	pryna!
dysgu (to learn)	dysga!
canu (to sing)	cana!
eistedd (to sit)	eistedda!
siarad (to talk/speak)	siarada!
edrych (to look)	edrycha!
darllen (to read)	darllena!
dweud (to say)	dweda!

● The noun which directly follows a command (the direct object) undergoes
a Soft Mutation:

Dysgwch Gymraeg!	Learn Welsh!
Darllenwch bapur!	Read a paper!
Pryna gar newydd!	Buy a new car!
Siarada Gymraeg!	Speak Welsh!
Cofia fi ati hi!	Remember me to her!

● There is sometimes a change of spelling in the command form:

gwrando ar	(to listen to)	gwrandewch!
		gwranda!
gadael	(to leave)	gadewch!
gadael i	(to let)	gad!
dweud	(to say)	dwedwch!
		dweda!
cyrraedd	(to arrive)	cyrhaeddwch!
		cyrhaedda!
aros	(to stop/wait)	arhoswch!
		arhosa!
cymryd	(to take)	cymerwch!
		cymera!
meddwl	(to think)	meddyliwch!
		meddylia!

● **Irregular verbs**

These are all different and have to be learnt individually. Here are the three most often used:

bod (to be)	byddwch	bydd/bydda
mynd (to go)	ewch (S.W.)/ cerwch (N.W.)	cer (S.W.)/ dos (N.W.)
dod (to come)	dewch (S.W.)/ dowch (N.W.)	dere (S.W.)/ tyrd (N.W.)

For example:

Byddwch yn blant da!	Be good children!
Bydd yn ofalus!	Be careful!
Bydda'n ofalus!	
Ewch/Cerwch mewn tacsi!	Go by taxi!
Dos/Cer i'r gwely!	Go to bed!
Dewch i mewn!	Come in!
Tyrd/Dere yma!	Come here!

● **Negative commands**

Peidiwch/Peidiwch â	(polite singular/plural)
Paid/Paid â	(familiar singular)

For example:

Peidiwch â siarad Saesneg!	Don't speak English!
Paid â siarad Saesneg!	Don't speak English!
Peidiwch â rhedeg ar y lawnt!	Don't run on the lawn!
Paid â rhedeg ar y lawnt!	Don't run on the lawn!

Technically, the preposition **â** should form part of this pattern, but it is often dropped in speech. If the **â** is used, notice the Aspirate Mutation:

Peidiwch â cherdded ar y lawnt!	Don't walk on the lawn!
Paid â phrynu sglodion!	Don't buy chips!

â becomes **ag** in front of a word which begins with a vowel:

Peidiwch ag eistedd wrth y ffenest!	Don't sit by the window!
Paid ag agor y ffenest!	Don't open the window!

3.7 Conjunctions

● **a** (and) is used in front of a consonant and **ac** in front of a vowel. Remember that **w** and **y** are vowels in Welsh:

bachgen a merch	car a bws
tŷ ac ysgol	oren ac afal

● **a** causes an Aspirate Mutation in words beginning with **c**, **p** and **t**:

ci a chath	papur a phensil
coffi a the	mam a thad

● Notice what happens in the following examples:

a + y/yr	a'r
y ci a y gath	y ci a'r gath
y tŷ a yr ysgol	y tŷ a'r ysgol

● **neu** (or) causes a Soft Mutation:

| ci neu gath | te neu goffi |
| bachgen neu ferch | coffi neu de |

3.8 Numbers

● Usually a singular noun follows numbers in Welsh:

| saith ci | seven dogs |
| naw bachgen | nine boys |

● There are masculine and feminine forms of the numbers 2, 3 and 4 and their use depends on the gender of the noun to which they refer:

dau afal (m)	two apples
dwy het (f)	two hats
tri llyfr (m)	three books
tair cadair (f)	three chairs
pedwar car(m)	four cars
pedair pêl (f)	four balls

● The numbers **pump** (five), **chwech** (six) and **cant** (hundred) drop the final consonant when they stand immediately in front of a noun:

pum potel	five bottles
chwe llwy	six spoons
can punt	hundred pounds

● Feminine nouns undergo a Soft Mutation after **un** (one) – except those nouns which begin with **ll** or **rh**:

| un gath | un fraich |
| un llwy | un bunt |

- Masculine nouns after **dau** (two) and feminine nouns after **dwy** (two) undergo a Soft Mutation:

dau gi (m)	two dogs
dwy gath (f)	two cats
dau dŷ (m)	two houses
dwy bont (f)	two bridges

- Masculine nouns undergo an Aspirate Mutation after **tri** (three):

tri char	three cars
tri thŷ	three houses
tri chap	three caps
tri phlentyn	three children

There is no mutation after **tair**, the feminine form for three.

- All nouns, masculine and feminine undergo an Aspirate Mutation after **chwe:**

chwe cheiniog	chwe chadair
chwe phlentyn	chwe phunt
chwe thŷ	chwe theisen

- Note the following:

deg (ten) becomes **deng** before **m**
deuddeg (twelve) becomes **deuddeng** before **m**
pymtheg (fifteen) becomes **pymtheng** before **m**
deng mlynedd ten years
deuddeng munud twelve minutes
pymtheng mis fifteen months

- **blynedd** (year) becomes **mlynedd** after many numbers although these numbers do not cause any other words to mutate nasally:

5	pum mlynedd
7	saith mlynedd
8	wyth mlynedd
9	naw mlynedd
10	deng mlynedd
12	deuddeng mlynedd
15.	pymtheng mlynedd
18	deunaw mlynedd
20	ugain mlynedd
50	hanner can mlynedd
100	can mlynedd

- When giving someone's age, whether male or female, remember to use the feminine forms **dwy** (two), **tair** (three) and **pedair** (four) which refer to the number of years, which is a feminine noun in Welsh:

Mae hi'n ddwy oed	She's two years old/of age
Roedd Gwyn yn bedair oed ddoe	Gwyn was four years old/ of age yesterday

- It is also possible to convey plurals by using a number followed by **o** followed again by the plural form of the noun:

tri o blant	three children
deg o geir	ten cars

In order to use this method of counting, it must be remembered that **o** causes a Soft Mutation, and that the plural form of the noun must be used. This can cause a problem as plural forms are irregular and do not follow any particular pattern.

3.9 Pronouns

3.9.1 Mutations and confirming pronouns

● See page 89 for full list of mutations

● All singular possessive pronouns cause mutations – (see section on mutations)

● Sometimes a confirming pronoun is used after the noun. This happens more often in the spoken language, but it can be omitted without affecting the meaning of a sentence. However, if the possessor needs to be emphasized, it is this confirming pronoun which is stressed in Welsh:

Dyma fy llyfr i a dacw dy lyfr di ar y bwrdd	Here's my book and there's your book on the table

● **fy** (my) is followed by an Nasal Mutation. The confirming pronoun for **fy** is **i**:

cath	fy nghath (i)	my cat
pen	fy mhen (i)	my head
trwyn	fy nhrwyn (i)	my nose
gardd	fy ngardd (i)	my garden
brawd	fy mrawd (i)	my brother
desg	fy nesg (i)	my desk

c, p, t, g, b and **d** are the only letters that mutate. Other letters remain unchanged:

ffrind	fy ffrind (i)	my friend
ysgol	fy ysgol (i)	my school
llaw	fy llaw (i)	my hand

● **dy** (your) and **ei** (his) cause a Soft Mutation. The confirming pronoun for **dy** is **di**. The confirming pronoun for **ei** (his) is **e** in South Wales and **o** in North Wales:

cath	dy gath (di)	ei gath (e/o)
	your cat	his cat
pen	dy ben (di)	ei ben (e/o)
	your head	his head
trwyn	dy drwyn (di)	ei drwyn (e/o)
	your nose	his nose
gardd	dy ardd (di)	ei ardd (e/o)
	your garden	his garden
brawd	dy frawd (di)	ei frawd (e/o)
	your brother	his brother
desg	dy ddesg (di)	ei ddesg (e/o)
	your desk	his desk
llaw	dy law (di)	ei law (e/o)
	your hand	his hand
rhosyn	dy rosyn (di)	ei rosyn (e/o)
	your rose	his rose
mam	dy fam (di)	ei fam (e/o)
	your mother	his mother

c, p, t, g, b, d, ll, rh and **m** and are the only letters that mutate. Other letters remain unchanged:

chwaer	dy chwaer (di)	your sister
nith	ei nith (e/o)	his niece

● **ei** (her) causes an Aspirate Mutation. The confirming pronoun for **ei** is **hi**:

cath	ei chath (hi)	her cat
pen	ei phen (hi)	her head
trwyn	ei thrwyn (hi)	her nose

c, p, and **t** are the only letters that mutate. Other letters remain unchanged:

brawd	ei brawd (hi)	her brother
gwaith	ei gwaith (hi)	her work

83

● **ei** (her) causes an **h** to appear before a vowel. (Remember that **w** and **y** are vowels in Welsh):

enw	ei henw (hi)	her name
acen	ei hacen (hi)	her accent

● The plural possessive pronouns **ein** (our), **eich** (your) and **eu** (their) do not cause mutations. But like **ei** (her), both **ein** (our) and **eu** (their) cause an **h** to appear before a vowel. The confirming pronoun for **ein** (our) is **ni**. The confirming pronoun for eich (your) is **chi**. The confirming pronoun for **eu** (their) is **nhw**:

ysgol	ein hysgol (ni)	our school
enw	eich enw (chi)	your name
iaith	eu hiaith (nhw)	their language

3.9.2 Pronouns and verb-nouns

● When a personal pronoun (me/you/him/her/it/us/them) is used immediately after a long verb (i.e. it is the object of that verb) then in Welsh we must also use the possessive pronouns (see 3.9 1 above) in front of the verb-noun.

● Remember that a long verb is one made up of the verb to be linked by **yn** or **wedi** to a verb-noun.

Fe/Mi fydda i'n ei ffonio hi heno	I will be telephoning her tonight
'Dyn ni ddim yn eu 'nabod nhw	We don't know them
Ydyn nhw wedi eich ateb chi?	Have they answered you?

● The possessive pronouns will cause the verb-nouns to undergo the mutations mentioned above:

She was reading it (the book – masc.) on the train	Roedd hi'n ei ddarllen e/o ar y trên
I can't hear you	Dw i ddim yn gallu dy glywed di
Does he love her?	Ydy e/o'n ei charu hi?

3.10 General Grammatical Points

3.10.1 Different meanings for words that are similar in English

● Note the difference between the following:

adref	home(wards)
gartref	at home
cartref	(a) home

For example:

Mae hi'n mynd adre ar ôl cinio	She's going home after lunch
Mae hi'n byw gartef	She lives at home
Mae cartre hyfryd gan Mair	Mair has a lovely home

● Note the difference between the following:

Cymraeg	Welsh (in language)
Cymreig	Welsh (pertaining to Wales)
Mae hi wedi prynu llyfr Cymraeg	She's bought a Welsh (language) book
Prynwch gig Cymreig	Buy Welsh meat

This happens with many words for languages and their cultures:

Language	Culture
Almaeneg	Almeinig
Saesneg	Seisnig
Ffrangeg	Ffrengig

● Note the difference between the following:

Cymru	Wales
Cymry	Welsh people

For example:

> Mae'r Cymry'n byw yng Nghymru   The Welsh live in Wales

● Note the difference between the following:

| 'nabod (from adnabod) | to know (a person/a place) |
| gwybod | to know (a fact) |

For example:

> Dw i ddim yn 'nabod y rheolwr   I don't know the manager but
> ond dw i'n gwybod ei enw e/o   I know his name

● Note the difference between the following

| Sut? | How? | (followed by a verb) |
| Pa mor? | How? | (followed by an adjective) |

For example:

> Sut roedd y tywydd yn Ffrainc?   How was the weather in France?
> Pa mor bell ydy Llundain o Fangor? How far is London from Bangor?

● Note the difference between the following:

| nôl | to fetch |
| yn ôl | back |

For example:

> Mae John wedi mynd i nôl y   John has gone to fetch the car
> car o'r garej   from the garage
> Mae'r llyfr wedi mynd yn ôl   The book has gone back to
> i'r llyfrgell   the library

Note: Both sound the same when spoken

● Note the difference between the following:

gwario	to spend money
treulio	to spend time

For example:

Mae Mair yn treulio ei gwyliau yn y siopau yn gwario arian	Mair is spending her holiday in the shops, spending money

3.10.2 Noun Clauses

● **bod** is used to convey 'that.....is/was' or 'that.....are/were' (this is called a noun clause):

Dw i'n gwybod bod John ar ei wyliau	I know that John is on holiday
Roedden nhw'n meddwl bod y plant yn chwarae yn y parc	They thought that the children were playing in the park

'that' is often left out in spoken English: I know John is on holiday

● **bod** has personal forms:

(fy) mod i	that I am/was
(dy) fod ti	that you are/were
(ei) fod o/e	that he is/was
(ei) bod hi	that she is/was
(ein) bod ni	that we are/were
(eich) bod chi	that you are/were
(eu) bod nhw	that they are/were

● In ordinary conversation the first pronoun is often omitted:

Dw i'n meddwl (fy) mod i'n mynd i Lundain yfory	I think that Im going to London tomorrow
Fe ddwedon nhw (eu) bod nhw'n rhydd (S.W.)/Mi ddudon nhw (eu) bod nhw'n rhydd. (N.W.)	They said that they were free
Dw i'n siŵr (ei) bod hi wedi mynd adre	I'm sure that she has gone home

● The **bod** pattern is also used after the following words

achos (because)	hwyrach/efallai (perhaps)
er (even though)	gobeithio (hopefully)

For example:

Mae Mair yn y gwely achos (ei) bod hi'n sâl	Mair's in bed because she is ill
Gobeithio (eu) bod nhw wedi ennill	Hopefully (I hope that) they have won

● When an emphatic sentence is used after that (i.e. the sentence begins with a noun or a phrase of some kind, not a verb), then the Welsh word for that is:

mai	(N.W.)
taw	(S.W.)

For example:

Mae Tom yn dweud mai/taw yn Nolgellau mae Mair yn byw	Tom says that it is in Dolgellau that Mair lives

3.10.3 Yes/No Replies

In Welsh we rarely use Yes and No – we actually use positive or negative forms of the verb. These are covered in the section on Verb. However, note the following:

● When an emphatic question is asked (i.e. the verb does'nt come first) the replies are always

Ie (S.W.)	Yes
Ia (N.W.)	
Nage (S.W.)	No
Naci (N.W.)	

For example:

Tîm pêl-droed Wrecsam enillodd?	Was it Wrexham soccer team
Ie/Ia	that won? Yes
Bethan ydy dy enw di?	Is your name Bethan? No, Elen
Nage/Naci, Elen	

3.11 Mutations

Soft Mutation			Nasal Mutation			Aspirate Mutation		
c	>	g	c	>	ngh	c	>	ch
p	>	b	p	>	mh	p	>	ph
t	>	d	t	>	nh	t	>	th
g	>	/	g	>	ng			
b	>	f	b	>	m			
d	>	dd	d	>	n			
ll	>	l						
rh	>	r						
m	>	f						

3.11.1 Soft Mutation

The Soft Mutation occurs:

● in singular, feminine nouns after the definite article **y** (the):

merch	y ferch	the girl
pêl	y bêl	the ball

The consonants **ll** and **rh** are an exception to this rule:

llaw	y llaw	the hand
rhaw	y rhaw	the spade

● in feminine nouns after the number **un** (one):

cath	un gath	one cat
basged	un fasged	one basket

● in feminine nouns after the number **dwy** (two):

cadair	dwy gadair	two chairs
merch	dwy ferch	two girls

● in masculine nouns after the number **dau** (two):

gwely	dau wely	two beds
ci	dau gi	two dogs

● in masculine and feminine nouns after the ordinal **ail** (second):

tŷ	yr ail dŷ	the second house (masc)
bachgen	yr ail fachgen	the second boy (masc)
merch	yr ail ferch	the second girl (fem)
desg	yr ail ddesg	the second desk (fem)

- when ordinals refer to feminine nouns, both the number and the noun will mutate:

y drydedd (the third)	y bedwaredd (the fourth)
y bumed (the fifth)	y chweched (the sixth)
y seithfed (the seventh)	yr wythfed (the eighth)
y nawfed (the ninth)	y ddegfed (the tenth)
y ddeuddegfed (the twelfth)	y bymthegfed (the fifteenth)
yr ugeinfed (the twentieth)	y ganfed (the hundredth)

For example:

y bumed ferch	the fifth girl
y ddegfed gân	the tenth song
y nawfed flwyddyn	the ninth year
y drydedd wobr	the third prize

- in adjectives which follow a singular, feminine noun:

merch dal	a tall girl
ffilm dda	a good film
gardd fawr	a large garden
cath fach	a small cat
ffrog goch	a red dress

- when the adjectives **hen** (old) and **hoff** (favourite) are placed before the noun and they cause the noun to undergo a Soft Mutation:

hen dŷ	an old house
hen gastell	an old castle
hoff fwyd	favourite food
hoff lyfr	favourite book

3 Beginners

- in adjectives after **gweddol** (fairly), **lled** (quite/fairly) and **rhy** (too):

yn weddol gryf	fairly strong
yn rhy denau	too thin
yn lled fyr	quite short
yn rhy galed	too hard

- after the prepositions **am** (at/for), **ar** (on), **at** (to/at), **dros** (over), **drwy** (through), **dan** (under), **wrth** (by), **o** (from), **i** (to), **heb** (without), **tan** (until), **gan** (by/from):

heb fwyd	without food
i Gaernarfon	to Caernarfon
o Fangor	from Bangor
wrth ddrws y ffrynt	by/at the front door

- after the personal possessive pronouns **dy** (your) and **ei** (his):

tad	dy dad	your father
mam	ei fam	his mother

- in adjectives and nouns (not verbs) after the linking word **yn**:

coch	yn goch	red
meddyg	yn feddyg	a doctor

- the consonants **ll** and **rh** are exceptions to this rule:

llwyd	yn llwyd	grey
rhad	yn rhad	cheap

- after **Dyma** (Here's/This is) and **Dyna/Dacw** (There's/That's):

cadair	Dyma gadair!	Here's a chair!
desg	Dyna ddesg Rhian!	There's/That's Rhian's desk!

● after the conjunction **neu** (or):

| te/coffi | te neu goffi | tea or coffee |
| wisgi/cwrw | wisgi neu gwrw | whisky or beer |

● in verb forms after **Fe/Mi**:

| Clywais i | Fe/Mi glywais i | I heard |
| Talan nhw | Fe/Mi dalan nhw | They'll pay |

● after the **rhaid** pattern:

| Mae rhaid i'r plant fynd i'r gwely'n gynnar | The children must go to bed early |
| Does dim rhaid iddi hi dalu'r bil trydan heddiw | She doesn't have to pay the electricity bill today |

● in negative forms of short verbs in the Past and Future Tenses – except those verbs which begin with **c**, **p** or **t**:

| Ddarllenais i ddim papur ddoe | I didn't read a paper yesterday |
| Welodd hi mo'r ffilm | She didn't see the film |

● in question forms of short verbs in the Past and Future Tenses:

| Ddarllenaist ti'r papur ddoe? | Did you read the paper yesterday? |
| Welodd hi'r ffilm? | Did she see the film? |

● in the indefinite object of short verbs in the Past and Future Tenses (i.e. the first word afer the subject):

| llyfr | Fe ddarllenais i lyfr da | I read a good book |
| car | Mi brynan nhw gar newydd y flwyddyn nesa | They'll buy a new car next year |

Note patterns such as:

mynd	Mi wnes i fynd	I went
talu	Mi wna i dalu	I'll pay
cychwyn	Wnaiff/wneith y car gychwyn?	Will the car start?

- with days of the week to convey on a certain day:

| dydd Mawrth | Tuesday |
| ddydd Mawrth | on Tuesday |

- when adverbial expressions of time are used in sentences:

| Fe briodon nhw ddwy flynedd yn ôl | They married (got married) two years ago |

- after **mor/cyn** (as) when comparing adjectives:

| tywyll | mor dywyll/ cyn dywylled | as dark |
| poeth | mor boeth/ cyn boethed | as hot |

- after the possession pattern based on **gan**:

| Mae gynno fo wallt du | He has/He's got black hair |

- in verb forms which convey the negative reply No (after the negating word **Na**), except those verbs which begin with **c**, **p** or **t**:

| Byddwn | Yes (we will be) |
| Na fyddwn | No (we won't be) |

● in verb-nouns after the **hoffwn** pattern (Affirmative and Question forms only):

Mi hoffwn i fynd	I'd like to go
Hoffen nhw gael?	Would they like to have?

● in verb-nouns after the **dylwn** pattern (Affirmative and Question forms only):

Mi ddylwn i fynd	I ought to/should go
Ddylen nhw gael?	Should they have?

● after **cyn** and **mor** when forming the equative degree of adjectives:

tal (tall)	cyn daled â (ag)	(as tall as)
creulon (cruel)	mor greulon â (ag)	(as cruel as)

● after **yn** when forming the comparative degree of adjectives:

tal (tall)	yn dalach na(g)	(taller than)
creulon (cruel)	yn fwy creulon na(g)	(more cruel than)

● in the superlative degree of the adjective when it refers to a feminine noun:

tal (tall) y tala	masculine
y dala	feminine

● in the noun used in indefinite sentences after the word '**na** (N.W.):

Mae 'na gi wrth y drws	There's a dog by the door

● immediately after a command:

Darllena lyfr!	Read a book!
Siaradwch Gymraeg!	Speak Welsh!

3.11.2 Nasal Mutation

The Nasal Mutation occurs:

● after the preposition **yn** (in):

Dolgellau	yn Nolgellau	in Dolgellau
Tonypandy	yn Nhonypandy	in Tonypandy

● **yn** changes to **ym** when the word which follows begins with **m** or **mh**:

Bangor	ym Mangor	in Bangor
parti Mair	ym mharti Mair	in Mair's party

● **yn** changes to **yng** when the word which follows begins with **ng** or **ngh**:

gardd Tom	yng ngardd Tom	in Tom's garden
car Bill	yng nghar Bill	in Bill's car

● after the personal pronoun **fy**:

car	fy nghar (i)	my car
pen	fy mhen (i)	my head
trwyn	fy nhrwyn (i)	my nose
gardd	fy ngardd (i)	my garden
brawd	fy mrawd (i)	my brother
desg	fy nesg (i)	my desk

3.11.3 Aspirate Mutation

The Aspirate Mutation occurs:

● in masculine nouns after the number **tri** (three):

car	tri char	three cars
pen	tri phen	three heads
tŷ	tri thŷ	three houses

● in all nouns, masculine and feminine, after the number **chwe** (six):

ceffyl	chwe cheffyl	six horses (masc)
plentyn	chwe phlentyn	six children (masc)
tŷ	chwe thŷ	six houses (masc)
ceiniog	chwe cheiniog	six pence (fem)
pêl	chwe phêl	six balls (fem)
teisen	chwe theisen	six cakes (fem)

Notice that we drop the final consonant **ch** in the number **chwech** when it is followed by a noun.

● after the conjunction **a** (and):

te/coffi	te a choffi	tea and coffee
coffi/te	coffi a the	coffee and tea
tatws/pys	tatws a phys	potatoes and peas
pys/tatws	pys a thatws	peas and potatoes
bara/caws	bara a chaws	bread and cheese
clust/trwyn	clust a thrwyn	ear and nose

● after the personal possessive pronoun **ei** (her):

tad	ei thad (hi)	her father
papur	ei phapur (hi)	her paper
car	ei char (hi)	her car

- after the following prepositions **â/gyda** (with), **tua** (towards or about/approximately):

siarad â/phlant	to talk to children
tua thri o'r gloch	about three oclock
torri gyda chyllell	to cut with a knife

- in the negative form of verbs in the Past Tense:

clywed	Fe/Mi glywais i	Chlywais i ddim
prynu	Fe/Mi brynodd Tom	Phrynodd Tom ddim
talu	Fe/Mi dalon nhw	Thalon nhw ddim

- in the negative form of verbs in the Short Future Tense:

clywed	Fe/Mi glywaf i	Chlywaf i ddim
prynu	Fe/Mi bryniff Tom	Phryniff Tom ddim
talu	Fe/Mi dalan nhw	Thalan nhw ddim

- after **â** (as):

mor swnllyd â pharot	as noisy as a parrot
mor bell â Phontypridd	as far as Pontypridd

- after **na** (than):

yn dalach na choeden	taller than a tree
yn oerach na Chanada	colder than Canada

- after **na** when forming negative replies (No):

Cewch!	Yes you may!
Na chewch!	No, you may not!

- after **â** in negative commands:

Peidiwch â chadw sŵn!	Don't make a noise!
Paid â phoeni!	Don't worry!

4

INTERMEDIATE/ HIGHER

4.1 Mutations

This information is additional to the information given on pages 89-98.
Soft Mutations occur:

● in direct objects of the short form verb:

| Ysgrifennais i lythyr | I wrote a letter |

● in nouns after adjectives:

| Unig blentyn ydy e | He's an only child |

● after the questions particle **A**:

| A fydd e'n dod i ginio? | Will he be coming to dinner? |

● after negative particle **Ni**, if it doesn't take an Aspirate Mutation:

| Ni ddes i adre' yn y car | I didn't come home in the car |

● after relative pronoun **a**:

| Dyma'r llyfr a brynais i ddoe | This is the book which I bought yesterday |

● after **pa** (which):

| Pa raglenni teledu wyt ti'n eu hoffi? | Which television programmes do you like? |

● after **pan** (when):

| Pan gwrddaist ti â John, oedd e'n iawn? | When you met John, was he all right? |

● after possessive **gan**, **gyda**, if it comes before the object:

| Mae gen i frawd a chwaer | I've got a brother and sister |
| Mae 'da fi frawd a chwaer | I've got a brother and sister |

● in all adverbs:

Es i i'r sinema ddoe	I went to the cinema yesterday
Es i yno bythefnos yn ôl	I went there a fortnight ago

Nasal Mutations occur:

● in **blynedd** and **blwydd** after 5, 7, 8, 9, 10 and any numeral including a form of 10 or 20:

Pum mlynedd yn ôl es i i Lundain am wythnos	Five years ago I went to London for a week
Mae hi'n ugain mlwydd oed	She's twenty years old

Aspirate Mutations occur:

● in nouns after **'i, 'w** (internal pronouns, her):

Mae'i thad yn gweithio yn y coleg	Her father works in the college

● after **tra** (extremely, while):

Roedd e'n dra chanmoliaethus	He was extremely complimentary

4.2 Sentence Patterns

Sentences perform five functions in Welsh:

● **Statements**

Prynodd y dyn y papur	The man bought the paper

● **Questions**

A brynodd y dyn y papur?	Did the man buy the paper?

● **Commands**

Prynwch y papur, ddyn	Buy the paper, man

● **Express wishes or desire**

O, na fyddai'n haf o hyd	Oh, that it were still summer

● **Exclamation**

Mor fawr yw e!	How great he is!

4.2.1 Statements

A number of types of sentence are used to make a statement:

● **Simple Sentence**

This is a sentence with one clause:

Cyrhaeddodd y dyn	The man arrived
Bydd Aled yn dod	Aled will come
Rydw i'n mynd i'r sinema	I'm going to the cinema

● **Compound Sentence**

A sentence with more than one clause linked with conjunctions such as **a, ond, neu**:

Daeth e i'r ystafell ac eisteddodd i lawr	He came to the room and sat down
Es i'r siop ond ni phrynais ddim	I went to the shop but didn't buy anything

● **Complex Sentence**

In such a sentence there is a main clause and a subordinate clause which provides further information about the main clause. These can do the work of:

an adjective:

Dyma'r dyn a brynodd y car	Here's the man who bought the car

a noun:

Rwy'n credu bod y bws wedi mynd	I think that the bus has gone

an adverb:

Aeth y plant adref pan ganodd y gloch	The children went home when the bell rang

● Mixed Sentence

Sometimes a word or a phrase will come before the verb for emphasis.
The relative pronoun **a/y/yr/sydd** is used between that being emphasised and the verb.

Hywel a enillodd	(It was) Hywel (who) won
Hywel sydd yn ennill	Hywel is winning
Yn y gwaith y cafodd e'r ddamwain	It was in work that he had the accident

The third person singular form of the verb comes after the relative pronoun (**a, y/yr**) no matter if the subject is singular or plural.

You will rarely, if ever, come across the next two types of sentence. If you are studying academic Welsh to a high level, you may come across them. They are:

● Abnormal Sentence

This is a very old form which is rarely used now, except in poetry. The structure is as above, though there is no emphasis:

Mi a welais	I saw
Ni a welsom	We saw

Note that the form of the verb corresponds to the subject.

● **Nounal sentence**

This is another very old form of sentence and is usually only seen in proverbs and sayings:

Hir pob aros	Every wait is long
Gwir pob gair	Every word is true
Nid aur popeth melyn	All that glitters is not gold

Note that there is no verb in this type of sentence.

4.2.2 Forming sentences

In Welsh sentences are formed in one of two ways:

● Form of to be   + person   + yn/'n   + predicate
   Rydw   **i**   **'n**   **mynd (i'r sinema)**
   I'm going to the cinema.

   Roedd   **hi**   **'n**   **bert**
   She was pretty.

● Add short form ending to stem of verb-noun:

Verb-noun	Stem	Ending	Verb
Yfed	**Yf-**	**odd** (he/she)	**Yfodd e** He drank
Gwylio	**Gwyli-**	**ais** (I)	**Gwyliais i** I watched

Short form verbs are described more fully in the section on verbs.

● **Emphatic sentence**

In the emphatic sentence, a stressed phrase or word comes before the verb.

Yn yr ysgol mae John heddiw	It is in school that John is today
Heddiw mae John yn yr ysgol	(It is) today John is in school
John ydy'r un sydd yn yr ysgol	John is the one (who's) in school

4.2.3 Relative/Adjectival clause

This type of clause is used to do the work of an adjective, and they describe the noun or pronoun in the main clause. The two parts of the sentence are linked by relative pronouns:

- **a/sydd**

When the noun is the subject, that is, doing the action, **a** is used with all forms of the verb except the present tense, when **sydd** or **sy'** is used:

Dyma'r dyn a ddaeth i'r parti	Here's the man who came to the party
Dyma'r dyn a oedd wedi bod i'r parti	Here's the man who had been to the party
Dyma'r dyn sydd yn dod i'r parti	Here's the man who is coming to the party

The form of the verb after the relative pronoun remains singular even if the subject is plural:

Dyma'r dynion a ddaeth i'r parti	Here are the men who came to the party

- **y/yr**

When either a personal prepostition, or a dependant pronoun is included in the clause that follows then **y/yr** is used:

Dyna'r dyn yr oeddwn am ei weld neithiwr	There is the man I wanted to see yesterdsay
Dyma'r ferch y clywais amdani	This is the girl I heard about

- **na**

Na (**nad** before vowels) is used in the negative, and there is an Aspirate Mutation or Soft Mutation:

Dyna'r dyn a ddaeth i'r parti	Dyna'r dyn na ddaeth i'r parti
Dyna'r dyn a welais i ddoe	Dyna'r dyn na welais i ddoe
Dyna'r dyn sy'n dod i'r parti	Dyna'r dyn nad yw'n dod i'r parti
Dyna'r dyn yr oeddwn yn ei weld ddoe	Dyna'r dyn nad oeddwn yn ei weld ddoe

4.2.4 Noun clauses

Look at the following sentences:

> Mae cyfrinach gyda fi   I have a secret
> The noun **cyfrinach** is the object
> Rydw i'n gwybod bod Aled yn priodi   I know that Aled is marrying

As **bod Aled yn priodi** fulfills the same function as **cyfrinach,** it is a noun clause.

● It's possible to replace Aled in the sentence with the pronoun **e**:

> Rydw i'n gwybod ei fod e'n priodi   I know that he's marrying

● Noun clauses always follow these phrases:

Mae'n rhaid	You must	Mae'n sicr	It's certain
Mae'n rhaid dweud	It must be said	Mae'n hysbys	It's known
Mae'n rhaid cyfaddef	It must be admitted	Mae'n drist	It's sad
Mae'n amlwg	It's obvious	Mae'n dda	It's good
Mae'n drueni	It's a pity	Mae'n annhebygol	It's unlikely
Mae'n wir	It's true	Mae'n debyg	It seems
Mae'n ffodus	It's fortunate	Dyna lwc	There's lucky
Dyna anffodus	There's unlucky		

● When the action in the noun clause is in the past tense, the verb-noun is used after the preposition **i**:

> Mae'n amlwg i mi orffen y gwaith   It's obvious that I finished the work
> Mae'n ffodus i ti orffen y gwaith   It's fortunate that you finished the work
> Dyna lwc i Aled orffen ei waith   There's lucky that Aled finished his work

● With other tenses, the noun clause is linked to the main clause with **y/yr**:

Bydd	Ydych chi'n meddwl **y** bydd Aled yn priodi?	Do you think that Aled will marry?
Bydd wedi	Mae'n siwr **y** bydd e wedi priodi erbyn hyn	It's certain that he will have married by now
Byddai	Dywedodd rhywun **y** byddai'n barod i helpu	Somebody said that she would be willing to help
Dod	Mae'n annhebygol **y** daw e nawr	It's unlikely that he'll come now
Gwneud	Rydw i'n credu **y** gwnai hi ysgrifenyddes dda	I think that she would make a good secretary

Note that in spoken Welsh, **y/yr** are very often omitted.

● The negative forms are **na/nad**:

PRESENT	nad ydw i	nad ydyn ni
	nad wyt ti	nad ydych chi
	nad yw e/hi	nad ydyn nhw
PAST	Mae'n debyg na phriododd Aled	It's seems that Aled did not marry

● Emphasis:

mai/taw is used if the noun clause is used to emphasise the main clause. The negative is **nad**:

Clywais i mai Hywel a enillodd	I heard that it was Hywel who won
Mae e'n dweud taw Dafydd oedd y gorau	He says that it was Dafydd who was best
Mae'n sicr, nad fi a ddywedodd wrtho	It's certain that it wasn't me who told him

4.2.5 Adverbial Clauses

Sometimes a whole clause is used to do the work of an adverb, that is, it gives us information about when, how or why something has happened/is happening/will happen, etc. These are adverbial clauses, and are linked to the action by conjunctions. Adverbial clauses are the subordinate clauses most often used, and there is a variety of ways of using them (**sm** denotes that a Soft Mutation occurs after the conjunction, and **am** denotes that an Aspirate Mutation occurs after the conjunction):

● Conjunction + verb

pan	when (sm)	Dewch yn ôl pan glywch y gloch	Come back when you hear the bell
er pan	since (sm)	Mae'n amser hir er pan enillon ni	It's a long time since we won
tra	while (am)	Eisteddwch tra bo'r prifathro'n siarad	Sit down while the headmaster is talking
pe	if (sm)	Pe bai'r arian gyda fi, ni fyddai problem	If I had the money, there would be no problem
os	if	Os daw hi nawr, gofynnwch iddi aros	If she comes now, ask her to wait
oni/onid	unless (am, sm)	Oni chaf ateb erbyn yfory, bydd hi'n rhy hwyr	Unless I get an answer by tomorrow, it will be too late
hyd oni	until (am, sm)	Dydw i ddim yn gallu dweud unrhywbeth hyd oni ddaw'r cadeirydd	I can't say anything until the chairman comes

- Conjunction + y/yr + verb

hyd y	until	Rhaid i mi aros hyd y daw	I must wait until he comes
pryd y	when	Aeth pawb yn dawel pryd y dechreuodd siarad	Everyone went quiet when he started speaking
fel y	so that	Aeth yn gynnar fel y gallai gael sedd dda	He went early so that he could have a good seat
fel y	as	Adnabyddais John fel y daeth i'r ystafell	I knew John as he came into the room
ble/lle y	where	Eisteddwch lle y mynnoch chi	Sit wherever you want

- Conjunction + verb-noun

trwy	by (sm)	Dechreuodd y gerdd trwy ddisgrifio'r bore	He started the poem by describing the morning
wrth	as (sm)	Clywais sgrech wrth fynd heibio'r ffenest	I heard a scream as I went past the window
wrth	by (sm)	Wrth ymarfer bob dydd, dowch yn rhugl	By practising every day you will become fluent
wedi	after	Byddaf yn gadael wedi pacio	I'll be leaving after packing
ar ôl	after	Roedden ni'n deall ar ôl clywed y ddarlith	We understood after hearing the lecture
er mwyn	in order to	Prynodd Siân bapur er mwyn darllen newyddion y dydd	Siân bought the paper in order to read the news of the day

● Some conjunctions fit into more than one of the above patterns:

nes/ hyd nes	until	Arhoswch yma hyd nes y dof i	Wait here until I come
		Arhosais nes cael ateb	I waited until I got an answer
cyn	before	Leanne, gorffennwch y gwaith cyn y daw Meic yn ôl	Leanne, finish the work before Meic comes back
		Gorffennwch hwn cyn mynd adref	Finish this before going home
erbyn	by the time	Bydd popeth yn barod erbyn y dôn nhw	Everything will be ready by the time they come
		Byddaf wedi blino erbyn heno	I'll be tired by tonight
rhag ofn	in case	Gwisgwch eich cot rhag ofn y daw i lawio	Wear a coat in case it rains
		Gwisgais i got rhag ofn iddi lawio	I wore a coat in case it rained

Gan, am, oherwydd, oblegid, achos, o achos because, and **er** although

● These conjunctions are used with:

y/yr + verb	Es i ddim allan oherwydd yr oeddwn yn gwybod eich bod chi'n dod	I didn't go out because I knew you were coming
bod	Rydw i'n gwybod hynny am fod John wedi dweud	I know that because John said so
i + object + verb-noun	Gan i mi golli'r bws, rhaid i mi gerdded	Because I've missed the bus, I must walk

To turn all of the above into negatives, use **na/nad** after the conjunction (literary Welsh) or **ddim** (oral form)

Ddaethon ni ddim am na chlywon ni'r gloch yn canu	We didn't come because we didn't hear the bell
Doeddwn i ddim yn gwybod hynny achos nad oedd John wedi dweud	I didn't know that, because John had not said

4.3 Genitive

This information is additional to the information given on pages 35-36. There is no possessive apostrophe in Welsh as in the English 'the Welshman's shoes'. The pattern in Welsh is:

esgidiau'r Cymro	literally: shoes the Welshman

That is, the thing which is 'possessed' comes first, followed by the 'possessor'. A useful method of forming the possessive is to convert the English into:

● the shoes of the Welshman

● then drop the first 'the' and the 'of'

● shoes the Welshman

● and translate this:

● **esgidiau'r Cymro**

Here are some more examples:

the man's car **car y dyn**	the car of the man	car the man
the girl's father **tad y ferch**	the father of the girl	father the girl
David's psalms **Salmau Dafydd**	the psalms of David	psalms David
on the horse's back **ar gefn y ceffyl**	on the back of the horse	on back the horse

| a leader of men
arweinydd dynion | a leader of men | leader men |
| the village square
sgwâr y pentref | the square of the village | square the village |

This pattern can be extended:

| car Mair | Mair's car |
| Beth yw lliw car Mair? | What is the colour of Mair's car? |

The pattern is used extensively with place names:

Abertawe	Aber Tawe	The mouth (of the river) Tawe
Llantrisant	Llan tri sant	The church of the three saints
Tyddewi	Tŷ Ddewi	The house of Saint David

4.4 Verbs

This information is additional to the information given on pages 37 onwards. The verb in Welsh exists in one of three moods, that is:

INDICATIVE, which expresses a fact or a statement
SUBJUNCTIVE, which expresses a wish or something conditional
IMPERATIVE, which expresses a command or strong desire

Usually, the verb has two forms, that is, in Welsh there are two ways of denoting an action:

● the long form, in which a form of the verb 'to be' is used with a verb-noun,

● the short form, where an ending is added to the stem of a verb-noun to create a discrete verb which shows person, action and tense.

Most short form verbs are regular, that is, they follow a regular and consistent pattern in each particular tense. The exceptions are:

mynd	to go	gwneud	to do
dod	to come	gwybod	to know
cael	to have	adnabod	to recognise

There are also a few **defective verbs** which need noting.

4.4.1 Verbs (long forms)

Bod – Present Tense

This information is additional to the information given on pages 37, 38, 39. Note that the Present Habitual is either formed by adding '**arfer**' between **yn** and the verb-noun, or by the Future Tense.

Mae Siân yn arfer mynd allan ar nos Wener	Siân usually goes out on a Friday night
Bydd Siân yn mynd allan ar nos Wener	Siân usually goes out on a Friday night

The 3rd Person Singular in the Present Tense needs particular attention because of the number of forms which exist. For example, there is no difference in meaning between **ydy**, **mae**, **sydd** and **oes** as they all originate from the same verb 'to be'. The difference lies in their use:

Mae is used:

● for statements:

Mae John yn mynd i'r sinema	John is going to the cinema

● after some question words:

| Ble mae John heddiw? | Where is John today? |

Ydy/Yw is used:

● for questions with definite objects:

| Ydy e'n mynd i'r dafarn? | Is he going to the pub? |

● with mixed sentences (for emphasis):

| John ydy f'enw i | My name is John |
| Prifathrawes ydy fy mam | My mother's a headmistress |

● with question words if followed by a noun/pronoun:

| Pwy ydy tad John? | Who is John's father? |
| Pwy ydy e? | Who is he? |

Oes is used:

● for questions where the object is indefinite:

| Oes bachgen yn yr ystafell? | Is there a boy in the room? |

sydd, sy' is used:

● with question words if followed by adjectives/verbs/adverbial phrases:

Pwy sy'n mynd i'r sinema heno?	Who's going to the cinema tonight?
Pwy sy'n ddrwg?	Who's naughty?
Beth sydd ar y llawr?	What's on the floor?

● with answers to the above pattern:

| Siân sy'n mynd i'r sinema heno | (It is) Siân (who) is going to the cinema tonight |
| John sy'n ddrwg | (It is) John (who) is naughty |

at the start of adjectival clauses:

| Dyna'r dyn sy'n dod yfory | There's the man who's coming tomorrow |

mai (**taw** in South Wales) is used in noun clauses for emphasis. Look at the following sentences:

| Hywel a enillodd | (It is) Hywel (who) won |
| Owain sy'n cynrychioli'r ysgol | (It is) Owain (who) is representing the school |

If the above are used as clauses rather than as independent sentences in their own right, **mai** needs to be used to link them to the main clause:

| Clywais i mai Hywel a enillodd | I heard that it was Hywel who won |
| Ydy e'n wir mai Owain sy'n cynrychioli'r ysgol? | Is it true that it is Owain who's representing the school? |

The negative of **mai/taw** is **nad**.

Bod – Past Tense

This information is additional to the information given on pages 57-58. It can also be used in these ways:

● to mean being somewhere, being ill, or acting in a certain way:

Bues i yno hefyd	I was there as well/I went there as well
Buon nhw yma neithiwr	They were here last night
Buodd John yn sâl am wythnos	John was ill for a week
Buon ni'n ffôl	We were foolish
Buoch yn garedig iawn	You were very kind

● to denote past tense in conjunction with another verb-noun:

| Bues i'n siarad â'r prifathro | I talked to the headmaster/ I was talking to the headmaster |

● in idiomatic phrases:

Buodd e farw	He died
Buodd rhaid iddo fynd ar unwaith	He had to go at once
Buodd damwain neithiwr	There was an accident last night

Bod – Future Tense

This information is additional to the information given on pages 37-40. The Future Tense can also be formed by using the Present Tense along with an adverb or adverbial phrase:

Mae Nia yn mynd i'r sinema heno	Nia is going to the cinema tonight

Bod – Other Tenses

PRESENT PERFECT	have/has	Use present + **wedi**	Mae e wedi gweld – He has seen
PRESENT PERFECT CONTINUOUS	have/has been	Use present + **wedi bod**	Dw i wedi bod allan – I've been out
IMPERFECT CONTINUOUS	used to	Use imperfect + arfer	Roedd hi'n arfer mynd – She used to go
PLUPERFECT CONTINUOUS TENSE	had been	Use imperfect + **wedi bod**	Roedd e wedi bod yng Nghaerdydd – He had been in Cardiff
FUTURE PERFECT	will have	Use future + **wedi**	Bydda i wedi gweld Siân – I will have seen Siân
FUTURE PERFECT CONTINUOUS	will have been	Use future + **wedi bod**	Byddwn ni wedi bod i'w gweld hi – We will have been to see her

Bod – Conditional.

This information is additional to the information given on pages 67-80.
Conditional forms occur in a number of phrases and idioms. In literary Welsh the
partical **Pe** precedes the **taswn e.g. Pe taswn, Petai** etc. The form
Petawn/Pe bawn etc. is also used to convey the Conditional Tense:

Cyn **bo** hir	Before long
Fel y **bo**'r galw	As the need arises
Pan **fo**	When there is
Lle **bo** angen	Where there's a need
Nes y **bôn** nhw'n cyrraedd	Until they arrive
Tra **bo** dau	While there are two
Pan **fwyf** yn hen	When I'm old
Pe **bawn** i	If I were to
Fel **petai**	As it were
Heb os nac oni **bai**	Without a doubt
Oni **bai** am	Apart from
Da **boch** chi	Goodbye

Bod – Imperative

This information is additional to the information given on pages 76-78. This
mood denotes a command or a strong desire, and short forms are dealt with
later in the Section. Here are some **bod** forms:

Byddwch yn dawel	Be quiet
Bydd yn wrol	Be brave
Boed hynny fel y bo	Be that as it may
A fo ben, **bid** bont	He who may be a leader, may he also be a bridge
Bydded yn ofalus	One must be careful

Na is used in the negative:

Na fyddwch drist	Don't be sad
Na fydded mor ffôl	Don't be so foolish

4.4.2 Verbs (short forms)

The first thing one must do when using short form verbs is to identify the stem to which the ending will be added. The 'categories' of verb-noun stems are:

● Verb-nouns where ending is dropped:

canu	sing	can
codi	rise	cod
cerdded	walk	cerdd
rhedeg	run	rhed
bwyta	eat	bwyt
egluro	explain	eglur
dychwelyd	return	dychwel
aredig	plough	ared
sefyll	stand	sef

● Verb-nouns where the stem is whole word:

eistedd	sit	eistedd
deall	understand	deall
dangos	show	dangos
darllen	read	darllen
chwerthin	laugh	chwerthin (chwardd)
cadw	keep	cadw
cyfaddef	admit	cyfaddef

● Verb-nouns where an element is added to make the stem:

addo	promise	addaw
gwrando	listen	gwrandaw
aros	wait	arhos
cynnwys	contain	cynhwys
cyrraedd	arrive	cyrhaedd
cynnal	hold	cynhali
trin	treat	trini
disgwyl	expect	disgwyli
newid	change	newidi
caniatáu	allow	caniateu
dechrau	begin	dechreu
amau	doubt	amheu
cau	shut	cae
arwain	lead	arweini
bygwth	threaten	bygythi
meddwl	think	meddyli
cyffwrdd (â)	touch	cyffyrdd (â)
ymweld (â)	visit	ymwel (â)
dianc	escape	dihang
gadael	leave	gadaw/gadew
ymadael (â)	take leave of	ymadaw (â)/ymadew (â)
dweud	say	dywed

4.4.3 Defective Verbs

Some verbs are called defective verbs, that is, they are limited to certain tenses and persons.

Dylwn

There are only two tenses to this verb now, the Imperfect and the Pluperfect:

Imperfect

Dylwn i	I should
Dylet ti	You should
Dylai e/Dylai o	He should
Dylai hi	She should
Dylai John	John should
Dylen ni	We should
Dylech chi	You should
Dylen nhw	They should

Pluperfect

Dylswn i	I should have
Dylset ti	You should have
Dylsai e/Dylsai o	He should have
Dylsai hi	She should have
Dylsai John	John should have
Dylsen ni	We should have
Dylsech chi	You should have
Dylsen nhw	They should have

For example:

Dylwn i fynd i weld fy nghyfaill	I should go to see my friend
Dylset ti dalu am y llyfr hwnnw	You should have paid for that book

● The Pluperfect is also conveyed by adding **fod wedi** to the Imperfect:

Dylet fod wedi talu am y llyfr hwnnw   You should have paid for that book

● **Ebr, Ebe, Eb**

These are the only forms of the verb, and are placed directly before the subject. They are used to quote the actual words spoken and are only used in literary Welsh:

'Dewch i mewn,' ebe'r dyn	'Come in,' said the man
'Diolch yn fawr,' ebe fi	'Thank you very much,' I said

● **Meddaf**

This verb is only used in the Present and Imprefect Tenses.

Present

Meddaf i	I say
Meddi di	You say
Medd e/o	He says
Medd hi	She says
Medd John	John says
Meddwn ni	We say
Meddwch chi	You say
Meddan nhw	They say

The Present Tense is used to express someone's ideas or opinions, for example:

Roedd hi'n gêm dda, meddan nhw	It was a good game, so they say
'Pwy, meddwch chi, yw'r gorau?'	'Who, would you say, are the best?'

Imperfect

Meddwn i	I said
Meddet ti	You said
Meddai e/o	He said
Meddai hi	She said
Meddai John	John said
Medden ni	We said
Meddech chi	You said
Medden nhw	They said

● The Imperfect is used instead of the Past Tense, in the same way as **ebe**:

'Dewch yma,' meddai'r dyn (dywedodd y dyn)	'Come here,' the man said
'Diolch yn fawr,' meddwn i (dywedais i)	'Thank you very much,' I said

● **Geni**

The only short forms of the verb-noun are the impersonal forms:

Genir	is/are born
Genid	was/were born over a period of time
Ganwyd/Ganed	was/were born
Ganesid	had been born

'To be born' is an idiomatic form in Welsh, using a form of **cael** in front of **geni**:

Ces i fy ngeni	I was born (Literally: I had myself a birth)
Cawson nhw eu geni	They were born (Literally: They had themselves a birth)

● **Gorfod**

Gorfod + verb-noun are used after a form of the verb 'to be' to convey the meaning of **rhaid** (must):

Dw i'n gorfod mynd nawr	I must go now
Wyt ti'n gorfod aros mewn heno?	Must you stay in tonight?

In the Past Tense you may see the following:

Gorfu i'r dringwyr droi yn ôl	The climbers had to turn back
Gorfu i mi wneud fy ngwaith cartref	I had to do my homework
Gorfu i ti weithio'n galed, do?	You had to work hard, did you?

4.4.5 Passive Voice

In Welsh we also call the passive voice the 'impersonal'. Orally, the idea is conveyed by **cael** (have):

Present	Mae'r car yn cael ei lanhau	The car is being cleaned
Future	Bydd y car yn cael ei lanhau	The car will be cleaned
Perfect	Mae'r car wedi cael ei lanhau	The car has been cleaned
Imperfect	Roedd y car yn cael ei lanhau	The car was being cleaned
Pluperfect	Roedd y car wedi cael ei lanhau	The car had been cleaned
Past	Cafodd y car ei lanhau	The car was cleaned
Future Perfect	Bydd y car wedi cael ei lanhau	The car will have been cleaned

However, there are verb endings which denote action and time but which do not give information about person(s) carrying out the action.

The endings are:

-id (imperfect)	Gwerthid llyfrau yma	Books were sold here (over a long period)
-wyd (past perfect)	Gwerthwyd llyfrau yma	Books were sold here
-ir (present/future)	Gwerthir llyfrau yma	Books are sold here

Here are some examples:

Mae'r gêm **yn cael ei chwarae** yfory	**Chwaraeir** y gêm yfory	The game **is being played** tomorrow
Rydyn ni'n cael ein dysgu gan Cennard	**Dysgir ni** gan Cennard	**We are being taught** by Cennard
Rydych chi'n cael eich ateb gan y Cadeirydd	**Atebir chi** gan y Cadeirydd	**You are being answered** by the Chairman
Mae'r canlyniad **yn cael ei gyhoeddi** am hanner nos	**Cyhoeddir** y canlyniad am hanner nos	The result **is being announced** at midnight

● You will find that the ending **-ir** causes a change of vowel in some verbs – usually an **'a'** becomes an **'e'**:

talu	tel	telir
canu	cen	cenir
siarad	siared	siaredir

Mae'r gweithwyr **yn cael eu talu** bob dydd Iau
Telir y gweithwyr bob dydd Iau.
The workers are (will be) paid every Thursday

● Most impersonal forms have a subject:

Cyhoeddir **y llyfr** yr wythnos nesa'	The book is being published next week
Agorir **y drysau** am 7 o'r gloch	The doors are being opened at 7 o'clock

But some impersonal forms stand independently:

Credir	It is believed
Gobeithir	It is hoped
Dywedir	It is said
Deëllir	It is understood

Credir bod y gêm wedi cael ei gohirio	**It is believed** that the game has been postponed
Credir bod dau ddyn wedi cael niweidiau difrifol	**It is believed** that two men have received serious injuries
Gobeithir cynnal parti	**It is hoped** to hold a party
Gobeithir dal y lladron yn fuan	**It is hoped** to catch the thieves quickly (soon)
Dywedir bod y tywydd yn mynd i wella	**It is said** that the weather is going to improve
Deëllir bod y plismyn wedi dal y lladron	**It is understood** that the policemen have caught the thieves

● Irregular verbs have impersonal forms:

cael	**ceir**	**cafwyd**
gwneud	**gwneir**	**gwnaethpwyd/gwnaed**
mynd â	**eir â**	**aethpwyd â**

Ceir tywydd poeth yn Florida	Hot weather **is (to be) had** in Florida
Cafwyd amser da gan bawb	A good time **was had** by all
Gwneir te ar ôl y pwyllgor	Tea **is made** after the committee meeting
Gwnaethpwyd (Gwnaed) llawer o arian yn y ffair	A lot of money **was made** in the fair
Eir â'r anifeiliaid i'r farchnad bob mis	The animals **are taken** to (the) market every month
Aethpwyd â'r dyn i'r ysbyty ar ôl y ddamwain	The man **was taken** to the hospital after the accident

● Other verbs are not exactly irregular – but they do have a slight irregularity in their personal forms:

cynnal	**cynhelir**	**cynhaliwyd**
rhoi (rhoddi)	**rhoddir**	**rhoddwyd**

Cynhelir pwyllgor nos Lun nesa'	A committee meeting **will be held** next Monday night
Cynhaliwyd y gêm er gwaetha'r tywydd	The game **was held** in spite of the weather
Rhoddir anrheg i bob plentyn	A present **is given** to every child
Rhoddwyd anrheg i bawb	Everyone **was given** a present

● To make negative statements – merely place **Ni** in front of the verb:

Ni siaredir Almaeneg yn Rwsia	German **is not spoken** in Russia
Ni atebwyd y cwestiynau	The questions **were not answered**

● **Ni** causes an Aspirate Mutation to verbs beginning with **c**, **p** and **t**:

Ni chafwyd enillydd	A winner **was not had** (no winner was found)
Ni chynhelir y pwyllgor nos yfory	The committee meeting **will not be held** tomorrow night
Ni phrynwyd car newydd	A new car **was not bought**
Ni thelir arian i'r plant	The children **are not paid** (any) money

4 Intermediate/Higher

- **Ni** causes a Soft Mutation in the other mutatable consonants

Ni welwyd y ffilm	The film **was not seen**
Ni ddaliwyd y lleidr	The thief **was not caught**
Ni roddir anrhegion	Presents **are not given**

4.4.6 Reflexive Verbs

By putting **ym-** before in front of certain verbs, it is possible to create new verbs where the person carrying out the action also receives the action (note the Soft Mutation):

dangos (show)	ymddangos (appear)	Dw i'n ymddangos heno	I'm appearing tonight
golchi (to wash something)	ymolchi (to wash ourself)	Ymolchais i am naw	I washed at nine

After some reflexive verbs, **â** precedes the object (**ag** before vowels). Note the aspirate mutation:

lladd (kill)	ymladd (fight)	Roeddwn i'n ymladd â fy chwaer drwy'r amser	I was always fighting with my sister
gweld (see)	ymweld (visit)	Dw i'n ymweld ag Alun	I'm visiting Alun
cymryd (take)	ymgymryd (undertake)	Mae e'n ymgymryd â'r gwaith	He's undertaking the work
gadael (leave)	ymadael (leave)	Roedd rhaid i mi ymadael â'r ysgol yn un ar bymtheg	I had to leave school at sixteen
gwneud (to do)	ymwneud (concerning)	Mae'r cwyn yn ymwneud â phlant Nia	The complaint is concerning Nia's children
gwrthod (refuse)	ymwrthod (reject)	Dw i'n ymwrthod â'ch barn chi	I reject your opinion

4.5 Nouns

There are different kinds of nouns in Welsh, in much the same way as English:

● Common nouns are names given to objects:

pêl ball   llyfr book   dinas city

● Proper nouns are names given to people, rivers, countries etc.:

Alun, Tawe, Cymru

● Concrete nouns are names given to objects with substance or are visible:

bwyd food   llyfr book   papur paper

● Abstract nouns are names given to concepts and abstracts:

cariad love   daioni goodness   hiraeth longing

● Collective nouns are names gives to collections of individuals:

tyrfa crowd   cynulleidfa audience

In Welsh, every noun must have a gender, no matter to which of the above categories it belongs. Unfortunately, there's no hard and fast rule about the gender of a noun. When you look up an English word in a Welsh dictionary, if you want to discover the gender look up the word in the Welsh section and it's gender will be noted. One of the following will be used, depending upon the dictionary you are using:

n.m.	noun, masculine
n.f.	noun, feminine
n.p.	noun, plural
e.g.	enw gwrywaidd (masculine noun)
e.b.	enw benywaidd (feminine noun)
e.ll.	enw lluosog (plural noun)

There are a few general pointers which can assist you:

- The gender of nouns which refer to living objects will sometimes be obvious:

llew	lion	llewes	lioness
Cymro	Welshman	Cymraes	Welshwoman
myfyriwr	student	myfyrwraig	student
tad	father	mam	mother

- Most nouns to do with weather are masculine (note that we use the feminine **hi** to describe the weather itself. This is because there is no neuter in Welsh: **Mae hi'n braf** It is fine)

- Most nouns to do with time are masculine

- Most nouns to do with matter are masculine

- Most verb-nouns are masculine

- Most nouns to do with geographical features are feminine

- Most nouns to do with trees are feminine

- Most nouns to do with illness are feminine

- Most collective nouns are feminine

- Some nouns will correspond to the gender of their subject:

  cariad boyfriend/girlfriend, **ffrind** friend, **perthynas** relative, **cymar** friend

These are only guidelines, and it is always best to check in the dictionary. However, note the following:

Mae hi'n wyth o'r gloch	It's eight o' clock
Mae hi'n heulog	It's sunny

4.5.1 Plurals

Most nouns in Welsh have a singular and a plural form, and the most common way of forming the plural is to add an ending. Once again, however, there is no simple solution to which word has which ending. There are seven ways of forming plurals:

● Add a plural ending **au, iau, ion, on, i, ydd, oedd, edd, ed, od, iaid**:

llong	llongau	llun	lluniau,	ysgol	ysgolion
cysur	cysuron	llestr	llestri	fforest	fforestydd
gwisg	gwisgoedd	dant	dannedd	merch	merched
menyw	menywod	estron	estroniaid		

● Change a vowel **a>ai, a>ei, a>y, e>y, o>y, w>y, oe>wy**:

brân	brain	car	ceir	alarch	elyrch
castell	cestyll	ffordd	ffyrdd	asgwrn	esgyrn
croen	crwyn				

● Combine the above:

mab	meibion	nant	nentydd	capten	capteiniaid
saer	seiri	maes	meysydd	cawr	cewri
traul	treuliau	awr	oriau	cwm	cymoedd

● Drop a singular ending:

mochyn	moch	pysgodyn	pysgod	llygoden	llygod
pluen	plu				

● Drop a singular ending and change a vowel:

hwyaden	hwyaid	deilen	dail	cneuen	cnau
dilledyn	dillad				

● Change a singular ending for a plural ending:

unigolyn	unigolion	cwningen	cwningod

- Change a singular ending for a plural ending and change a vowel:

teclyn taclau	cerdyn cardiau	miaren mieri

- Some nouns do not have a plural form, for example:

tywydd	weather	gwres	heat	llwch	dust
baw	dirt	te	tea	coffi	coffee
ewyn	foam	llaeth	milk	eira	snow
bara	bread				

- Some nouns have only plural forms:

gwartheg	cattle	pigion	selections
gweddillion	remainder, balance		

4.6 Adjectives

This is dealt with in Section 3.3. In addition:

- some adjectives can come before the noun:

annwyl	dear	gwir	true
hen	old	gau	false
unig	only	hoff	favourite
cam	mis-	cas	least favourite
gwahanol	different	prif	chief, main
newydd	new	eithaf	quite
llawn	high, full	prin	scarcely, barely

They all cause a soft mutation except **eithaf.**

- Some adjective only come before the noun:

ambell	occasional	amryw	several
cryn	moderate	cyfryw	such
dirprwy	deputy	holl	all, complete
rhyw	some	unrhyw	any
ychydig	few	y fath	such, kind
peth	some	pob	every
rhai	some	sawl	several

They all cause a Soft Mutation except **peth**, **pob**, **rhai** and **sawl**.

- it's possible to put any adjective before the noun, but this is a poetic style:

y glas fôr	the blue sea
y brydferth ferch	the pretty girl

- the position of an adjective can change meaning:

unig blentyn	only child
plentyn unig	lonely child
gwir angen	a real need
angen gwir	a true need
hen gadair	an old chair
cadair hen	a very old chair
cas bethau	hated things
pethau cas	nasty things
cam argraff	wrong impression
llwybr cam	a crooked path
hoff nofelydd	favourite novelist
nofelydd hoff	dear novelist
gwahanol rannau	various parts
rhannau gwahanol	different parts

● Adjectives can be modified by adding the following:

MODIFIER	POSITION	MUTATION	EXAMPLE	ENGLISH
eithaf/eitha	before	–	eithaf teg	quite fair
digon	before	–	digon teg	fair enough
go	before	soft	go dda	quite good
gweddol	before	soft	gweddol dawel	fairly quiet
hollol	before	soft	hollol deg	entirely fair
cwbl	before	soft	cwbl dywyll	totally dark
perffaith	before	soft	perffaith hedd	perfect peace
rhy	before	soft	rhy ddrud	too expensive
tra	before	aspirate	tra charedig	rather kind
iawn	after	–	da iawn	very good
braidd	after	–	hwyr braidd	rather late
braidd yn	before	soft	braidd yn hwyr	rather late
dros ben	after	–	da dros ben	extremely good
gwirioneddol	before	soft	gwirioneddol beryglus	really dangerous
hynod	before	soft	hynod ddiolchgar	most thankful
cymharol	before	soft	cymharol ddrud	relatively expensive
pur	before	soft	pur wael	quite poor
lled	before	soft	lled dda	fairly good

● Repeating adjectives can modify them:

Redd yr ysgol yn fawr, fawr	The school was very big
Cerddais yn araf, araf at y deintydd	I walked very slowly to the dentist

● Some modifiers are used with **yn** before the adjective:

ychydig yn rhy fach	a little bit too small
braidd yn hen	rather old
tipyn yn fawr	a bit large

● Formerly, adjectives had to correspond to the gender or number of the noun. Feminine nouns required feminine adjectives and plural nouns required plural adjectives. Though no longer a grammatical rule, it is still to be found in certain forms.

byr	short	stori fer	short story
gwyn	white	torth wen	white loaf
melyn	yellow	het felen	yellow hat
crwn	round	bord gron	round table
du	black	mwyar duon	blackberries
byr	short	straeon byrion	short stories

● However, the rule still applies in the case of **arall/eraill** (other):

plentyn arall	other child
plant eraill	other children

4.6.1 Irregular Adjectives

This is dealt with in Section 3.3.2. Some adjectives do not follow the patterns noted in that section

POSITIVE	EQUATIVE	COMPARATIVE	SUPERLATIVE
da good	cystal	gwell	gorau
drwg bad	cynddrwg	gwaeth	gwaethaf
mawr bad	cymaint	mwy	mwyaf
bach small	cyn lleied	llai	lleiaf
hir long	cyhyd	hwy	hwyaf
cynnar early	cynted	cynt	cyntaf
uchel high	cyfuwch	uwch	uchaf
hawdd simple	cyn hawsed	haws	hawsaf
hen old	cyn hyned	hŷn	hynaf
llydan wide	cyfled	lletach	lletaf
anodd difficult	cyn anhawsed	anos	anhawsaf
isel low	isel	is	isaf
ieuanc young	ieuenged	iau	ieuaf/ieuengaf
agos close	agosed	nes	nesaf/agosaf

4.7 Personal Pronouns

4.7.1 Dependent Personal Pronouns

● The dependent personal pronoun describes the noun, that is, it cannot be used unless it is linked to an object. The forms are:

fy	my	(causes nasal mutation)
dy	your	(causes soft mutation)
ei	his	(causes soft mutation)
ei	her	(causes aspirate mutation)
ein	our	
eich	your	
eu	their	

● After the prepositions **i** to, **gyda** with, **â** with, **o** from, **tua** towards, a shortened form is used:

'm	my	
'th	your	(causes soft mutation)
'i, 'w	his	(causes soft mutation)
'i, 'w	her	(causes aspirate mutation)
'n	our	
'ch	your	
'u, 'w	their	

4.7.2 Independent Personal Pronouns

mi, fi, i	I, me
ti, di	you
ef, fe, e, fo, o	he, him
hi	she, her
ni	we, us
chi	you
nhw	they, them

These pronouns are used in a number of ways:

● As the subject of a sentence, or in place of the noun:

Dewch gyda ni	Come with us
Gwelodd e fi yn y coleg	He saw me in college

● As a completion of personal forms of the verb:

Rydw i
Gwelaist ti
Bydd e
Roedd hi
Buon ni
Oeddech chi...?
Aethon nhw

● When showing possession (the genitive), in oral Welsh pairs of pronouns are used, one either side of the object:

fy... i	fy nhad i	my father
dy... di	dy gar di	your car
ei... e	ei gi e	his dog
ei... hi	ei chath hi	her cat
ein... ni	ein llyfr ni	our book
eich... chi	eich coleg chi	your college
eu... nhw	eu brawd nhw	their brother

4.7.3 Demonstrative Pronouns

Masculine		Feminine	
hwn	hwnnw	hon	honno
this (one)	that (one)	this (one)	that (one)

● When referring to abstract nouns the following is usually used:

hyn	hynny
this (one)	that (one)
y rhain	y rheini
these	those

Examples:

Mae hyn yn wir	This is true
Mae'r llyfr hwnnw'n perthyn i John	That book belongs to John
Mae hon yn un dda	This is a good one
Ble mae'r rheina'n mynd?	Where are those going?

4.7.4 Reflexive Pronouns

fy hun	fy hunan
dy hun	dy hunan
ei hun	ei hunan
ein hun	ein hunain
eich hun	eich hunan/eich hunain
eu hun	eu hunain

● Reflexive pronouns are used for emphasis:

| Roedd John ei hunan yn y dafarn | John himself was in the pub |
| Gwelais i Nia fy hunan | I saw Nia myself |

● They are used as objects to a verb:

| Gwelon nhw eu hunain ar y teledu | They saw themselves on television |
| Mwynhewch eich hunain! | Enjoy yourselves! |

4.8 Adverbs

An adverb modifies a verb, telling us how, why, when, where or to what extent an action takes place. As in English, most adverbs are formed from adjectives (quick > quickly).

● **yn** is used to turn adjectives into adverbs, in much the same way as the English suffix **-ly**. It causes a soft mutation, except in words beginning with **ll** and **rh**:

Diolch **yn fawr**	Thank you very much
Os gwelwch **yn dda**	Please (lit. If you see fit)
Mae'n bwrw glaw **yn drwm**	It's raining heavily
Mae e'n chwarae rygbi'**n dda**	He plays rugby well
Dw i'n teimlo'**n hapus** heddiw	I feel happy today

● **yn** is used with the comparative degrees of comparison:

Rwyt ti'n edrych yn well heddiw	You look better today
Mae'n gobeithio na fydd e'n waeth 'fory	He hopes that he's not worse tomorrow

● **yn** is omitted when the equative and superlative degrees of comparison are used adverbially:

Mae Siân wedi gwneud cystal â'i brawd	Siân has done as well as her brother
Gareth sy'n gallu canu orau	(It is) Gareth (who) can sing the best

● There are many adverbs in Welsh which occur naturally and are not formed from adjectives, for example:

heno	tonight	Dw i'n mynd allan heno	I'm going out tonight
eleni	this year	Es i i Sbaen eleni	I went to Spain this year
llynedd	last year	Aethon ni i Gernyw y llynedd	We went to Cornwall last year
ymlaen	on	Dewch ymlaen!	Come on!
ddoe	yesterday	Es i i'r gwaith ddoe	I went to work yesterday

● Nouns can be used adverbially:

Ble oeddet ti ddydd Sadwrn?	Where were you (on) Saturday?
Wyt ti'n mynd ar wyliau'r flwyddyn nesaf?	Are you going on holiday next year?

● **pob** (every) can be used to form adverbial phrases:

bob dydd	every day
bob amser	every time/always
bob blwyddyn	every year

As these are being used as adverbs they will take a soft mutation.

● There are two words which correspond to the English home, one is a pure adverb (**adref**), the other is a noun which can be used as an adverb (**gartref**):

Roeddwn i gartref neithiwr	I was at home last night
Aeth e adref am saith	He went home at seven

● Prepositions can be used to form adverbial phrases:

Roeddwn i gartref drwy'r nos neithiwr	I was at home all night last night

4.9 Prepositions

This information is additional to the information given on pages 32-36. This is additional information.

● Some verbs are followed by particular prepositions:

â

cytuno â	agree with
dod â	bring
mynd â	take
siarad â	speak to
ymweld â	visit
cwrdd â	meet
peidio â	stop (to cease)

am

aros am	wait for
cofio am	remember about
chwerthin am	laugh about
	(note: **chwerthin am ben** laugh at)
disgwyl am	expect
gwybod am	know about
holi am	ask about
meddwl am	think about
ymladd am	fighting for, fighting about
breuddwydio am	dream about
gofalu am	take care of

ar

blino ar	tire of
bodloni ar	be satisfied with
edrych ar	look at, watch
gweddïo ar	pray to
gwrando ar	listen to
sylwi ar	take notice of
ymosod ar	attack
galw ar	call upon
dibynnu ar	depend upon
gwenu ar	smile at
syllu ar	to gaze/stare at
tywynnu ar	shine upon

at

anfon at	send to (a person)
ysgrifennu at	write to
mynd at	go to (a person)

i

addo i	promise to
caniatáu i	allow
dangos i	show
gofyn i	ask
diolch i	thank
perthyn i	belong to
llwyddo i	succeed in

wrth

dweud wrth	to tell
adrodd wrth	relate to

yn

cydio yn	grasp/join
ymddiried yn	trust

● Some prepositions, when they are followed by a pronoun, will conjugate. Sometimes this will be accompanied by a vowel change:

wrth

wrtho i	wrthon ni
wrthot ti	wrthoch chi
wrthi hi	wrthyn nhw
wrtho fe	

heb

hebddo i	hebddon ni
hebddot ti	hebddoch chi
hebddi hi	hebddyn nhw
hebddo fe	

rhwng

rhyngo i	rhyngon ni
rhyngot ti	rhyngoch chi
rhyngddi hi	rhyngddyn nhw
rhyngddo fe	

yn

yno i	ynddon ni
ynot ti	ynddoch chi
ynddi hi	ynddyn nhw
ynddo fe	

drwy

drwyddo i	drwyddon ni
drwyddot ti	drwyddoch chi
drwyddi hi	drwyddyn nhw
drwyddo fe	

at

ata i	aton ni
atat ti	atoch chi
ati hi	atyn nhw
ato fe	

gan

gen i	gynnon ni
gennyt	gynnoch chi
ganddi hi	ganddyn nhw
ganddo fe	

dros

droso i	droson ni
drosot ti	drosoch chi
drosti hi	drostyn nhw
drosto fe	

o

ohono i	ohonon ni
ohonot ti	ohonoch chi
ohoni hi	ohonyn nhw
ohono fe	

i

i mi	i ni
i ti	i chi
iddi hi	iddyn nhw
iddo fe	

mo

mo is used in negative sentences where the object to short forms of the verb (past and future tenses) is definite:

Welais i mohono fe	I didn't see him

mohono i	mohonon ni
mohonot ti	mohonoch chi
mohoni hi	mohonyn nhw
mohono fe	

● Some prepositions conjugate by placing a pronoun between their two elements:

ar draws (across)

ar fy nhraws i	ar ein traws ni
ar dy draws di	ar eich traws chi
ar ei thraws hi	ar eu traws nhw
ar ei draws e	

ar ôl (after)

ar fy ôl i	ar ein hôl ni
ar dy ôl di	ar eich ôl chi
ar ei hôl hi	ar eu hôl nhw
ar ei ôl e	

● Similarly:

yn lle	instead
o gwmpas	around
o flaen	in front
ar gyfer	on behalf of/for
er mwyn	for the sake of
ar bwys	near
yn erbyn	against
wrth ochr	by the side of
o amgylch	around
yn ymyl	near

5

IDIOMS & PHRASES

5 Idioms & Phrases

5.1 Commands

Agorwch y drws	Open the door
Agorwch y ffenestr	Open the window
Arhoswch funud	Wait a minute
Byddwch yn dawel	Be quiet
Byddwch yn ofalus	Be careful
Caewch y drws	Close the door
Caewch y ffenestr	Close the window
Daliwch ati	Keep at it
Dewch i mewn	Come in
Dewch yma	Come here
Dewch ymlaen	Come on
Dos ymlaen (N.W.)	Go on
Eisteddwch	Sit down
Ewch adre	Go home
Ewch allan	Go outside
Ewch i nôl	Go fetch
Ewch ymlaen	Go on, go ahead
Ewch yn ôl	Get back, go back
Gadewch i ni fynd	Let's go
Hidiwch befo (N.W.)	Never mind
I ffwrdd â chi	Off you go, away with you
Os gwelwch yn dda	Please
Paid!	Don't! (Informal, singular)
Peidiwch!	Don't! (Formal, plural)
Peidiwch ag anghofio	Don't forget
Siaradwch yn arafach	Speak more slowly
Taw!	You don't say!
Tawelwch!	Silence!

5.2 Idioms

Ar agor	Open
Ar fai	To blame
Ar frys	In a hurry
Ar fy mhen fy hun	By myself, on my own
Ar gau	Closed
Ar hyn o bryd	At the moment
Ar unwaith	At once
Ar y dechrau	At the beginning
Ar y pryd	At the time
Beth bynnag	Anyway, however
Bwrw'r Sul	Spend the weekend
Byth a beunydd	Always, regularly
Byth a hefyd	Often, regularly, time and again
Byth eto	Never again
Canu'r piano	Play the piano
Cyn bo hir	Before long
Dal ati	Stick to it, continue
Dan ei sang	Full to overflowing
Dim eto	Not yet, not again
Dod i ben	Come to an end
Dod o hyd i	Come across
Dros ben llestri	Over the top, excessive
Dros y Sul	Over the weekend
Er gwaethaf	Despite, in spite of
Er hynny	Nevertheless
Er mwyn	For the sake of
Gan bwyll	Take it easy, wait a moment
Gwneud cawl o bethau	To make a mess
Hanner dydd	Midday, noon
Hanner nos	Midnight
Heb os nac onibai	Without a shadow of a doubt
Hwn a'r llall	One person and another
Hwyrach	Perhaps
Hyn a'r llall	This and that
Igam ogam	Zigzag
I'r dim	Exactly
Ling-di-long	Slowly
Lol botes maip	Utter rubbish
Lladd gwair	Cut the grass, mow the lawn
Mae arna i bunt i John	I owe John a pound
Mae cywilydd arna i	I'm ashamed
Mae chwant arna i	I have a desire

Mae chwant bwyd arna i	I'm hungry
Mae eisiau cot newydd arna i	I want a new coat
Mae hiraeth arna i	I have a longing
Mae'n braf arna i	It's fine with me, things are fine with me
Mae'n galed arna i	It's tough/hard on me
Mae'n debyg	It seems
Mae'n draed moch arna i	I'm in a mess
Mae'n dda gyda fi	I'm glad
Mae'n ddrwg gyda fi	I'm sorry (apology)
Mae'n flin gyda fi	I'm sorry (sympathy)
Mae'n gas gyda fi	I hate
Mae'n well gyda fi	I prefer
Mae ofn arna i	I'm afraid
Mae syched arna i	I'm thirsty
Malu awyr	Talking nonsense
Man a man i mi (S.W.)	I may as well
Newydd sbon	Brand new
Oddi wrth	From
O ddrwg i waeth	From bad to worse
O gam i gam	Step by step
Oherwydd	Because
O leiaf	At least
O'r diwedd	At last
O'r gorau	Very well
Rhoi i gadw	Put by, put away
Pam lai?	Why not?
Pedwar ban y byd	Four corners of the world
Rhoi'r ffidil yn y to	Give up
Rydw i wrth fy modd	I'm delighted, in my element
Sefyll arholiad	Sit an examination
Tamaid i aros pryd	Snack
Tân ar fy nghroen	Nuisance
Tipyn bach	A little bit
Un tro	Once, once upon a time
Unwaith	Once, once upon a time
Wedi'r cwbl	After all
Wedyn	Afterwards
Weithiau	Sometimes
Wrth gwrs	Of course
Ych a fi!	Ugh!
Yn aml	Often
Yn erbyn	Against
Yn lle	Instead of
Yn ymyl	Near

5.3 Greetings, Farewell and Feelings

Beth sy'n bod?	What's the matter?
Blinedig	Tired
Blwyddyn Newydd Dda	Happy New Year
Croeso	Welcome, You're welcome
Cyfarchion	Greetings
Diolch	Thank you
Diolch yn fawr	Thank you very much
Dydd da	Good day
Dymuniadau gorau	Best wishes
Gweddol	Fair
Hwyl	Cheerio
Hwyl fawr	Cheerio
Iechyd da!	Cheers! Good health!
Llongyfarchiadau	Congratulations
Nadolig Llawen	Merry Christmas
Pen-blwydd hapus	Happy birthday
Pob hwyl	All the best
Pob lwc	Good luck
Sut hwyl?	How are things?
Sut mae pethau?	How are things?
Sut mae'r hwyl?	How are things?
Sut wyt ti ers talwm?	How are you after this long time?
Wedi blino'n lân	Tired out
Wyt ti'n well?	Are you better?
Ydych chi'n well?	Are you better?

5.4 Weather

Mae'n arllwys y glaw	It's pouring with rain
Mae'n berwi	It's boiling
Mae'n boeth ofnadwy	It's terribly warm
Mae'n bwrw hen wragedd a ffyn	It's raining cats and dogs
Mae'n grasboeth	It's scorching
Mae'n gynnes	It's warm
Mae'n dwym uffernol	It's hellishly warm/hot
Mae'n dywydd garw	It's rough weather
Mae'n dywyll iawn	It's very dark
Mae'n ddiflas dros ben	It's very miserable
Mae'n ddiwrnod gwlyb	It's a wet day

Mae'n niwlog	It's misty
Mae'n oer uffernol	It's hellishly cold
Mae'n ofnadwy	It's terrible
Mae'n olau iawn	It's very bright/light
Mae'n arllwys y glaw	It's pouring down
Mae'n rhewi	It's freezing
Mae'n taranu	It's thundering
Mae'n uffernol	It's hellish

5.5 Comparisons

Fel coes brws	As dull as a brush
Mor dywyll â'r fagddu	Pitch black
Mor ddistaw â'r bedd	As quiet as the grave
Mor gyflym â mellten	As quick as lightning
Mor llawen â'r gog	As happy as a cuckoo
Yn canu fel aderyn	Singing like a bird
Yn crio fel babi	Crying like a baby
Yn goch fel gwaed	As red as blood

6

VOCABULARY

6 Vocabulary

6.1 Adverbs and Adverbials

The following adverbs and adverbial phrases have soft mutations where relevant, and can be used in sentences. For adverbs in compound and complex sentences, look in the Grammar section.

ar hyn o bryd	at the moment
ar ôl hynny	after that
bob blwyddyn	every year
bob dydd	every day
bore 'fory	tomorrow morning
drannoeth	the day after tomorrow
drwy'r dydd	all day
ddeng mlynedd yn ôl	ten years ago
ddoe	yesterday
echdoe	the day before yesterday
eleni	this year
heddiw	today
heno	tonight
llynedd	last year
nawr	now
nos yfory	tomorrow night
o'r diwedd	at last
pan	when (note: **pan** is never used as a question word)
prynhawn yfory	tomorrow afternoon
un tro	once, once upon a time
wedyn	later, afterwards
weithiau	sometimes
y flwyddyn nesaf	next year
y bore 'ma	this morning
yfory	tomorrow
ymhen ychydig	in a little while
y mis diwethaf	last month
y mis hwn	this month
y mis nesaf	next month
yn aml	often
y prynhawn yma	this afternoon
yr wythnos ddiwethaf	last week
yr wythnos hon	this week
yr wythnos nesaf	next week

6.2 Adjectives

agos	close
annwyl	dear
anodd	difficult
araf	slow
arall	other (note: plural form, eraill) .
bach	small, little
blasus	tasty
brown	brown
brwnt	dirty
byr	short
caled	hard
caredig	kind
cas	nasty
coch	red
creulon	cruel
crwn	round
cryf	strong
cul	narrow
cyflym	fast, quick
cyfoethog	rich
cyfforddus	comfortable
cyffredin	ordinary, common
cyffrous	exciting
cymylog	cloudy
cynnar	early
da	good
diddorol	interesting
diflas	miserable
doeth	wise
drwg	bad, naughty
du	black
dwfn	deep
ffiaidd	foul, despicable
ffyrnig	fierce
galluog	able
garw	rough
glas	blue
glân	clean
gofalus	careful
golau	light (colour/shade, not weight)
golygus	handsome

gwan	weak
gwerthfawr	valuable
gwlyb	wet
gwyn	white
gwyrdd	green
hagr	ugly
hapus	happy
hawdd	simple
hen	old
heulog	sunny
hir	long
hoff	favourite
hwyr	late
hyll	ugly
ifanc	young
iach	healthy
isel	low
llonydd	still, calm
llwyd	grey
llydan	wide
mawr	large, big
meddal	soft
melyn	yellow
newydd	new
oer	cold
ofnadwy	terrible, awful
oren	orange
pell	far
perffaith	perfect
pinc	pink
piws	puce (dark purple)
prif	main, chief, head
poeth	warm
porffor	purple
pwysig	important
rhad	cheap
swnllyd	noisy
sych	dry
syth	straight
tal	tall
tawel	quiet
tebyg	similar, alike
teg	fair

tenau	thin
tew	fat
tlawd	poor
tlws	pretty
trist	sad
trwm	heavy
twp	stupid
uchel	high
unig	only, lonely
ysgafn	light (weight)

6.3 Time

Dyddiau	**Days**
Dydd Llun	Monday
Dydd Mawrth	Tuesday
Dydd Mercher	Wednesday
Dydd Iau	Thursday
Dydd Gwener	Friday
Dydd Sadwrn	Saturday
Dydd Sul	Sunday

Gwyliau	**Holidays and Festivals**
Calan Gaeaf	Hallowe'en
Calan Mai	May Day
Dydd Calan	New Year's Day
Dydd Gŵyl Ddewi	St. David's Day
Dydd San Folant	Valentine's Day
Dydd Santes Dwynwen	Saint Dwynwen's Day
Gwener y Groglith	Good Friday
Gŵyl San Steffan	Boxing Day
Nadolig	Christmas
Nos Galan	New Year's Eve
Noswyl Nadolig	Christmas Eve
Y Pasg	Easter
Pen-blwydd	Birthday, Anniversary
Pen-blwydd priodas	Wedding anniversary
Priodas	Wedding, marriage
Y Sulgwyn	Whitsun
Sul y Mamau	Mothering Sunday
Sul y Pasg	Easter Sunday

Misoedd	Months
Ionawr	January
Chwefror	February
Mawrth	March
Ebrill	April
Mai	May
Mehefin	June
Gorffennaf	July
Awst	August
Medi	September
Hydref	October
Tachwedd	November
Rhagfyr	December

Tymhorau	Seasons
Gwanwyn	Spring
Haf	Summer
Hydref	Autumn
Gaeaf	Winter

Unedau amser	Units of time
awr	hour
bore	morning
blwyddyn	year
canrif	century
chwarter awr	quarter of an hour
deuddydd	two days
degawd	decade
dydd, diwrnod	day
echdoe	two days ago
eiliad	second
hanner awr	half an hour
mis	month
munud	minute
noson	night
noswaith	evening
oes	age
penwythnos	weekend
prynhawn	afternoon
pythefnos	fortnight
tri chwarter awr	three quarters of an hour
tridiau	three days
wythnos	week

6.4 Food

afal	apple
afu (S.W.)	liver
bacwn	bacon
banana	banana
bara	bread
blodfresych	cauliflower
brecwast	breakfast
brechdanau	sandwiches
bresych	cabbage
cacen	cake
cawl	soup, stew
cawl cennin	leek stew
caws	cheese
cig	meat
cig eidion	beef
cig moch	bacon
cig oen	lamb
cnau	nuts
cinio	dinner
coffi	coffee
creision	crisps
creision brecwast	breakfast cereal
creision ŷd	corn flakes
crempog	pancake
cwpan	cup
cwrw	beer
cyllell	knife
cyw iâr	chicken
chwisgi	whiskey
disglen	bowl, saucer
dŵr	water
eog	salmon
ffa	beans
ffa pob	baked beans
fforc	fork
ffrwythau	fruit
gwin	wine
halen	salt
hufen	cream
hufen iâ	ice cream
iau (N.W.)	liver

llaeth	milk
llefrith (N.W.)	milk
llwy	spoon
llysiau	vegetables
marjarîn	margarine
mefus	strawberries
mêl	honey
meipen	swede
menyn	butter
moron	carrots
mwyar duon	blackberries
nionod (N.W.)	onions
olew	oil
oren	orange
owns	ounce
paced	packet
padell	pan
padell ffrio	frying pan
panas	parsnips
peren	pear
pice ar y maen	Welshcakes
porc	pork
potel	bottle
pupur	pepper
pwys	pound (in weight)
pys	peas
pysgod	fish
saws	sauce
selsig	sausages
sglodion	chips
siocled	chocolate
sosban	saucepan
sudd oren	orange juice
swper	supper
tatws	potatoes
te	tea
tebot	teapot
tegell	kettle
teisen	cake
winwns (S.W.)	onions
wy	egg

6.5 World of Work

actor	actor
actores	actress
adeiladwr	builder
arlunydd	artist
athrawes	teacher (female)
athro	teacher (male)
awdur	author
awdures	author (female)
awyren	aeroplane
banc	bank
banciwr	banker
bardd	poet
bws	bus
cadeirydd	chairperson
cais	application
cantores	singer (female)
canwr	singer (male)
ceisio am swydd	applying for a job
cemegydd	chemist (industrial)
cigydd	butcher
clerc	clerk
clinig	clinic
cogydd	chef, cook
coleg	college
colli swydd	lose a job
cyfarwyddwr	director
cyfweliad	interview
chwaraewr pêl-droed	football player
chwaraewr rygbi	rugby player
chwaraewr tennis	tennis player
darlithydd	lecturer
disgybl	pupil
di-waith	unemployed
doctor	doctor
dyn camera	cameraman
dyn sain	sound man
dyn tân	fireman
ffatri	factory
fferyllydd	chemist, pharmacist
ffotograffydd	photographer
ffurflen gais	application form

gardd	garden
garddwr	gardener
glöwr	miner
gohebydd	correspondent
gorsaf	station
gwaith	work
gweinidog	minister
gweithio	work
gwerthwr	salesman
gwraig tŷ	housewife
heddwas	policeman
meddyg	doctor
lori	lorry
llawfeddyg	surgeon
maes awyr	airport
mecanig	mechanic
milwr	soldier
morwr	seaman
myfyriwr	student (male)
myfyrwraig	student (female)
newyddiadurwr	journalist
nyrs	nurse
paentiwr	painter, decorator
paffiwr	boxer
peilot	pilot
peiriannydd	engineer
pensaer	architect
plastrwr	plasterer
plismon	policeman
plymwr	plumber
postmon	postman
pobydd	baker
prifathrawes	headmistress
prifathro	headmaster
prifysgol	university
pwll glo	coal-mine
rhaglennydd	programmer
rheolwr	manager
saer	carpenter
siopwr	shopkeeper
swydd	job, position
swyddfa	office
swyddi	jobs

tacsi	taxi
tafarn	pub
tafarnwr	publican
teiliwr	tailor
trên	train
trydanwr	electrician
theatr	theatre
wedi ymddeol	retired
ymddiswyddo	resign
ysbyty	hospital
ysgol	school
ysgrifennydd	secretary (usually of a club, society etc. and can be male or female)
ysgrifenyddes	secretary

6.6 Places

Aberdaugleddau	Milford Haven
Aberhonddu	Brecon
Abergwaun	Fisguard
Abertawe	Swansea
Aberteifi	Cardigan
Amwythig	Shrewsbury
Ariannin	Argentina
Awstralia	Australia
Awstria	Austria
Bryste	Bristol
Caer	Chester
Caerdydd	Cardiff
Caeredin	Edinburgh
Caerfaddon	Bath
Caerfyrddin	Carmarthen
Caergaint	Canterbury
Caergrawnt	Cambridge
Caerhirfryn	Lancaster
Caerliwelydd	Carlisle
Caerloyw	Gloucester

Caerlŷr	Leicester
Caerwrangon	Worcester
Caerwynt	Winchester
Caerwysg	Exeter
Casnewydd	Newport
Cernyw	Cornwall
Croesoswallt	Oswestry
Cymru	Wales
Dulyn	Dublin
Dyfnaint	Devon
Dinbych	Denbigh
Dinbych y Pysgod	Tenby
Caerefrog	York
Ewrop	Europe
Ffrainc	France
Gwlad Belg	Belgium
Gwlad Groeg	Greece
Gwlad Pwyl	Poland
Gwlad yr Haf	Somerset
Henffordd	Hereford
Hwlffordd	Haverfordwest
Iwerddon	Ireland
Lerpwl	Liverpool
Llanllieni	Leominster
Lloegr	England
Llundain	London
Llwydlo	Ludlow
Llydaw	Brittany
Manceinion	Manchester
Môn	Anglesey
Prydain Fawr	Great Britain
Rhydychen	Oxford
Sbaen	Spain
Swisdir	Switzerland
Ynys Manaw	Isle of Man
Ynys Wyth	Isle of Wight
Ynys yr Iâ	Iceland
Yr Aifft	Egypt
Yr Alban	Scotland
Yr Almaen	Germany

Yr Eidal	Italy
Yr Iseldiroedd	Holland
Yr Unol Daleithau	The United States

There are many places names, such as Canada, India, Lichtenstein etc. where the English and the Welsh are the same.

6.7 Family

achau	genealogy
anti	aunty
bachgen	boy, son
brawd	brother
brawd yng nghyfraith	brother-in-law
cefnder	cousin (male)
coeden achau	family tree
cyfnither	cousin (female)
cyn-ŵr	ex-husband
cyn-wraig	ex-wife
chwaer	sister
chwaer yng nghyfraith	sister-in-law
dyweddïo	become engaged
ewythr	uncle
gefaill	twin
gefeilliaid	twins
gŵr	husband
gwraig	wife
hen dadcu	great grandfather
hen famgu	great grandmother
llyschwaer	stepsister
llysdad	stepfather
llysfab	stepson
llysfam	stepmother
llysferch	stepdaughter
llysfrawd	stepbrother
mab	son
mab yng nghyfraith	son-in-law
mam	mother
mamgu (S.W.)	grandmother

mam yng nghyfraith	mother-in-law
merch	daughter
merch yng nghyfraith	daughter-in-law
modryb	aunty
nai	nephew
nain (N.W.)	grandmother
nith	niece
pen-blwydd	birthday
pen-blwydd priodas	wedding anniversary
plant	children
plentyn	child
priodas	wedding
priod	married
priodfab	groom
priodferch	bride
priodi	to marry
tad	father
tadcu (S.W.)	grandfather
tad yng nghyfraith	father-in-law
taid (N.W.)	grandfather
teulu	family
wncwl (S.W.)	uncle
ŵyr	grandson
wyres	grand-daughter
ysgariad	divorce
ysgaru	to divorce

6.8 Weather

arllwys	pouring
braf	fine
bwrw	precipitating
bwrw cesair	hailing
bwrw eira	snowing
bwrw glaw	raining
cawod	shower
cawodydd	showers
crasboeth	scorching hot
cwmwl	cloud
cymhedrol	fair

cymylau	clouds
cymylog	cloudy
diflas	miserable
golau	light.
gwlyb	wet
gwynt	wind
gwyntoedd	winds
gwyntog	windy
haul	sun
heulog	sunny
hyfryd	lovely
llonydd	still
mellt a tharanau	thunder and lightning
oer	cold
oerfel	coolness
ofnadwy	terrible
pistyllu	pouring
rhew	ice
rhewi	freezing
rhynnu	freezing
storm	storm
stormus	stormy
sych	dry
torheulo	sunbathe
twym	warm
tywyll	dark
ysgafn	light

Index

Am wybodaeth am holl gyhoeddiadau'r Lolfa,
mynnwch gopi o'n Catalog newydd,
neu hwyliwch i mewn i'n gwefan:
www.ylolfa.com